MW01295334

WORTH THE PAIN

My Journey from Meth to Ministry

Jessica Youngblood

DISCLAIMER

This book is not rated PG or even PG-13. There are not fluffy, sugar coated stories within it. This is the real and raw story of my past and if you are the mother to a young girl, **PLEASE READ IT FIRST.** In the book, I share the love of Jesus Christ and the hope that my life has found through Him.

THANK YOU

I would like to thank my husband, Jonathan Youngblood! Babe, you have truly been my rock for almost 15 years. You have been my biggest supporter in anything God has called me to do, including this book. I truly wouldn't have completed this if it wasn't for you believing in me. I love you so much!

Daddy,

"Has anyone told you that they loved you lately?" This is how you told me you loved me. "Sacrifice" is the word that comes to mind when I think of you. You gave it all to raise me. Love is what I saw at every basketball game because no matter how hard you worked that day, you were standing on the sideline watching me play. You let me figure out this thing called life, but you also made one of the hardest decisions a parent has to make. The decision to give tough love. When I was so far into drugs, you told me that you couldn't be there for me. Though at the time I didn't understand, now I know it was actually the best thing you could have done in that moment. Daddy, you were the only consistent piece of my life. So, my rock bottom was having my choices push you away. But when your prodigal daughter returned home, your house was open and your love hadn't changed. I just want you to know that the world needs more dads like you. Ones that will rise up and take care of their families! I'm sorry that I always focused on what I was missing instead of appreciating what was right in front of me! Love you, Daddy! This is my thank you. For it all!

TABLE OF CONTENTS

FORWARD

The way Jessica shares her phenomenal story of deep pain and life-changing freedom is transformational. Her depth and uncensored vulnerability points to the healing power of Jesus Christ.

Whether you are stuck in a cycle of addictive habits or you need hope in any situation you are facing, this book is a gift that will remind you that there is no pit too deep or too dark that Jesus cannot rescue you from. I believe as you read Worth the Pain, chains that have been holding you captive for generations will be broken by the power of God's presence that is all over each page.

This is a book that I could not put down until I finished. I believe in Jessica Youngblood and I believe in her book. First-hand, I have seen her live out freedom daily and encourage everyone she meets to do the same.

- Pastor Oneka McClellan

INTRODUCTION

I wrote this book for the lady that is hopeless in a hotel room who wants to end her life. I wrote this for the drug addict that wants to give up because she can't overcome the addiction. I wrote this for the rich business woman who looks perfect on the outside, but is hollow on the inside. I wrote this for the twelve-year-old girl who thinks the world is out to get her. The book is for the broken. If you are in your religious bell tower looking for something to judge, you probably shouldn't read this book. Or maybe you should so you will see there is more to Jesus than religion.

This story isn't about any one individual. Names have been changed and stories have been blended for privacy. This wasn't written to run anyone into the ground or to air out my dirty laundry. It has taken me seven years to write this book. Throughout the first four years, I would turn on the computer, start thinking of my past, and would quickly shut it down because I realized that it would effect who I had become. I wasn't ready. I still had a lot of learning and growing to do. I still had a lot of wisdom to collect, so that I could share it with you. My first priority in life, my ministry, is being a good wife and mother. I couldn't have done those two things well had I written this book seven years ago.

As life has moved forward, I still knew that I was called to write. I became a pastor and my eyes were really opened to how broken the world is and how it needs hope. I strongly felt in this last year that the time was now! No matter the cost, I had to get this story on paper. So that is what I have done. And through it all, God has transformed me even more. He dove even deeper into my soul to pull out raw feelings and real pain.

When I began to write, God brought me a girl name Krista. She and I went for coffee and she shared how she was a writer. I immediately I thought I needed a "ghost writer." I wanted her to re-write what was done and add imagery and backstory. That is all fine and well, but I become so dependent on what I thought she had to do for me, so I put unrealistic expectations on her. I expected her to see this calling through to the end, but it wasn't her calling, it was mine. It was my job to stay up late to write. It was my job to ride places with my husband, laptop in hand, typing until my fingers cramped. So I went back to Krista and thanked her for lighting a fire in me and for showing me that I could write this book. So I took what she had helped me do and made it mine.

You see, I always kept telling God I couldn't do it because I wasn't a writer. He has reminded me time and time again that I am not a writer like everyone else. He doesn't call the equipped. No, He equips those who He calls. Frankly, I was kind of lazy and wanted someone else to do the work for me and that just wasn't going to fly anymore. So for two months I wrote nonstop. The more I wrote, the more I began to see it come to life! I put a table of contents together and had a photoshoot for the cover. But the closer I got to the end I knew I needed an angel to take my run-on paragraphs (yes, I mean paragraphs) and make them in to sentences, before it could go to the editor. And as always, God had a way even though I didn't see it. I looked up and she was right there in my life. My friend, Holly Moon, asked me if she could help me structure it before it went to the editor. My initial answer was "No! I want to keep our friendship." I said that because I knew if I said "yes" life would come at her hard and it would put a lot of pressure on our friendship. That is how the enemy works. When you walk out your calling, the enemy comes at you with the fullest force. We'll take more about that later in the book. Anyway, she is from Arkansas, like me, and we don't take "no" for an answer. She insisted that God told her to do it. That conversation happened on October 27, 2017. She started the first chapter the next day. I am writing the disclaimer on November 30, 2017 and she has one chapter left. Y'all, she add structure and grammar to my book in 33 days. This bad boy has taken me seven years to get on paper, but the rest has happened so fast, I can hardly believe it. I can't believe it is in your hands this very moment.

One

I LOVED IT

The first hit was amazing. It burned as it slid down the back of my throat, and then, euphoria. A rush like never before. The hairs on my head stood up. I could feel my eyes dilating and bulging out. The tingles went from the top of my head to the bottoms of my feet. My mind was as clear as it had ever been. I fell in love with those little white lines. It was one of the best things I had ever tried. It was my first hit of meth and it was like nothing I had ever experienced. What I didn't know was this drug would grip me like a python, and it was going to suck the last breath out of my lungs.

I needed to get high because nothing else was taking my hurt and pain away. So, one day, I was snorting as much as I could, trying to smoke every last drop in the pipe. At first, nothing seemed to be happening, but then it did. My heart started racing and my body sweating. It felt like a car was on my chest and I couldn't breathe. In that moment, I thought that was the end of my life and I didn't even care. I was overdosing and my body was shutting down. But, for the first time in a while, I thought of my son. I thought of his sky blue eyes and sandy blonde hair. I could see his smile and hear his laugh. I started screaming on the inside, "Wait, wait! I don't want to die like this! I don't want to be remembered as a meth addict with sores all over my body and my face sunken in!" You see, my son was about to turn one. And even though he didn't know it, his own mother was getting ready to die, not getting ready for his party.

Laying there in that bed, looking up to the ceiling, I was helpless. I realized that I ended up becoming the one person I didn't want to be: my mother, abandoning her child. A long time ago, I made a promise to myself that I would never become her.

I judged her and hated her for the pain she caused me. But, for the first time, in that moment, I had an ounce of forgiveness for my mom. I felt compassion for her story. I thought about the life I was living. How did I get here when I said I would never become this? It was supposed to be just a little at a party. I just wanted to try meth once, but it led to this. The truth is, this overdose was just an outward reflection of how dead I was on the inside. I was dead inside way before I let this drug control me. See, the drug was just a symptom of my internal battle and struggle that I had been dealing with my whole life.

In this book, I hope you take it all in. I pray you don't take this as another religious, weak book, but as a declaration that God still transforms people's lives and raises them from the dead. You can call me a modern day Lazarus.

John 11:21 NLT; Martha told Jesus, "Lord if only you had been here my brother would not have died."

I am sure you have had these moments in your life when you blame God for not saving you or rescuing you from the abuse or pain.

John 11:23 NLT- Jesus said to her, "Your brother will rise again."

That's what I am telling you. You will rise again if you don't give up. I was once dead in my own internal grave, but still breathing externally. But, today I am alive and well! I broke out of the prison walls that once trapped me! I am sharing the raw and real of my life and journey. In it is abandonment, rejection, emptiness, brokenness, hopelessness, and self-pity. My life could have ended so many times, but God's plan and purpose for my life was for me to rise so I could tell the world. I want you to know God has the same for you. No matter what you have been through, it's no excuse to stay stuck in your misery. I promise, His grace is enough.

Two
WHERE IT ALL BEGAN
PART I

Let me set the scene for you, because my story started long before I was even born. I'll start with my hometown, then I'll tell you about my family.

If you examine a map of Arkansas, it is made up of a few decent sized towns, but mostly tiny ones that you can drive right through and not even notice. The little ole' town where I grew up, Kirby, Arkansas, is a little country town with a population of a whopping 786 people. They may have reached 800 by now. So, as you can imagine, Kirby didn't have much, but as you drive into town on Highway 27 you will see my humble Alma Mater, Kirby High School. Home of the Trojans! Maroon and gray all day! We lived for high school basketball, maybe because it was the only sport we had. There were 32 students in in my graduating class and being such a small town, we were like family. Some days we hated each other, but most days we loved each other. Ahhh, the memories. Further into town, you will come up to the cutest little country store, Ernie Dunlap's, where we could get ice cream for a nickel. Ernie's was family owned and operated and the best place in town to hear the latest gossip. In the front of the store, there were a few tables where you could sit to eat your ice cream or have a soda. They were always occupied by a few old men talking about the weather and discussing current events. Everyone in town shopped at Ernie's. Even if you didn't have money, you could get what you needed and pay later. Across the street from Ernie's was the little post office and the local restaurant with the best home cooking around (it may have been the only restaurant, but it was still the best).

That is Kirby, Arkansas. But, there is one more place to tell you about: Teague

Hill. The hill was steep and rocky, but on top of it sat a humble little home. My home. Built by the hands of my dad and uncle, it was nothing fancy but we had everything we needed. And this is where it all began! The early years of my life, years that shaped me and molded me into who I am today. To be clear, this is through my eyes, my thoughts, and my feelings. This is not about what is true, not true, or what we believe the truth is! This story is not intended to damage any person or focus on any person except myself, and my perception only. For this reason, some names and locations might be changed to protect identities; but this story is true and the pain was most definitely real.

So, to tell you about my family, my daddy's name is Jerry Teague and he was a handsome "looker" back in his prime. He had that James Dean hair style, a perfectly clean-shaven face, and big brown eyes that could pierce right through you. He was the hardest working man I knew, whether it was driving a semi-truck across the country, chopping down trees in the fields, or spending his nights rebuilding motors in his shop for neighbors in need. Born and raised in Kirby, he had a loving mother and father and being the youngest of ten siblings, you can bet he was spoiled rotten. Shortly after graduating in 1972, he met my mom. My mother was a classic beauty and as my dad would say, "a sight for sore eyes." Her crystal blue eyes and silky black hair made her effortlessly beautiful. Behind all that beauty was pain and struggle and anything but a fairy tale. When she met my dad, she was pregnant with my brother, Bobby. I can just imagine my sweet daddy falling in love with this beautiful woman who was pregnant with another man's baby ("awww" sound effects here).

After just a few months of dating (and before my brother was born), they were married. They moved around a bit, but ended up back in Kirby and moved in with my great grandma, Edna, while they got on their feet. Just six months after having my brother, my mother was pregnant with me. My birth story is probably the best one you have heard in a while. My mom went into labor just after supper on August 27th. They rushed out the door, leaving my infant brother with Grandma as my dad hurried my mom into his old Pontiac to rush to the hospital. On the way there, they had to stop several times. Luckily, they made it to the hospital, but only to the parking lot. She had progressed quickly by the time they pulled in, and I guess I couldn't wait any longer to make my debut! So, in the back seat of that 1969 Pontiac, I was born on August 28, 1980. My dad ran inside the hospital and yelled, "My baby is having my wife... I mean... My wife is having my baby... in the car!" The thought of my mild tempered, calm dad, who probably didn't run very much, sprinting into the hospital and yelling frantically still makes me laugh. What a way to come into the world in that hospital parking lot in Hot Springs, Arkansas.

I always wonder what life for my parents was like during that time. Was it peaceful? Were they happy? Was it hard? Did they fight or did they love? I think about an old Polaroid picture, my mom cradling me in one arm, and Bobby in the other. He was feeding me with a bottle and she was gazing down at us. Me with a full head of black hair, wearing a white dress, only a couple of weeks old. Seeing her smile as she held tight her healthy (beautiful) children, I can't help but to imagine anything less than happiness, love, and peace.

After a few months of living with my grandma, my dad had saved up enough to move us out on our own. He was so proud of his beautiful little family and worked day and night to make sure we were never without. Mom spent her days looking after us the best she could, but her own demons began to creep in and take hold of her mind. I am sure she tried to ignore the dark thoughts. I am sure she tried to pretend as if she was fine, to hold on for her two children. But the question remained, could she make it through this? Or would she end up doing exactly what her mother did to her?

PART II

a·ban·don·ment

(a) To give up to the control or influence of another person or agent
(b) to give up with the intent of never again claiming a right or interest in[1]

This one word defined my life. It is the reason my life was one train wreck after another. It was the root of all of my issues. I was abandoned. I was my mother's personal responsibility, but it was too much on her so she walked out. The sad thing is, she wasn't the only one in the first 10 years of my life that would just walk out and never look back. The effect this had on me was extreme. Looking back now, I can see that I struggled with post-traumatic stress and it went unnoticed for a lot of years. It is crazy to think that the things in my childhood could cause psychological problems as if I had been to war. That is exactly how it felt my whole life; like I was on the front lines of a battlefield with no protection and the world was just taking its cheap shots at my heart.

Have you ever been abandoned? By parents or grandparents? Maybe a boyfriend or girlfriend? Has someone walked out of your life completely with no explanation? Don't worry, you're not alone. This has been on the rise since the 1970's. In 2002, 30 percent of homes in America were single parent homes. Y'all, that is 1.9 billion broken families with children who begin to carry the blame and search for their identity and worth outside the home.

It was May 1981, and per usual, my Grandma Edna was working around house. When she heard a noise out on the front porch, she ignored it at first and went on about her business. She was a tough woman and nothing seemed to bother her. A few minutes later she heard it again. This time, she went closer to the front door. She looked out the window and to her surprise, there was an infant car seat. She rushed outside and looked to see a beautiful baby girl. Her big blue eyes were red from crying and she looked as if she hadn't been bathed in days. Taped to the car seat was a note: "I can't do this anymore." That baby was me.

My dad was left to raise two small children and pick up the pieces, while barely hanging onto himself. He was never the same. We would beg to be close to him, even pile up into his bed at night when we were scared. He was afraid something would be said about abuse if he was too close to us. So his own fear left me feeling abandoned all over again. Even if one parent leaves, you can still feel the same effects from the one that stayed.

Although he had lots of help after my mom left, there was a huge hole in his heart. He was grateful for the support from his family. His dad, my Grandpa Albert, lived just across the field in the house where Dad grew up. Grandpa was one of my favorite people. Every day after school, Bobby and I would run across the field with the horses and Grandpa would be standing on the porch waiting for us. Always dressed for work in his plaid shirts and overalls, he would ride us around on the horses and tell us stories about what the world was like when he was our age. When we weren't playing in the pastures, Grandpa let us play video games on his Nintendo. I could play the snake game for hours; it was my favorite.

Aunt Nona and Uncle Lloyd lived just up the road. I loved going to visit them and they treated me like their own daughter. Their house was my safe-haven, so warm and full of love. No one ever turned down Aunt Nona's homemade biscuits with chocolate gravy. Even with the mess I made, she would let me laugh, play, and eat to my heart's content. Every year at Christmas, the whole house was decorated with tinsel and lights and a tree full of homemade ornaments that we made throughout the years. It might have been a little over the top, but to me it felt like home, especially after my mom left. Aunt Nona was the one to watch us for days at a time when my dad would take to the road driving the big rig.

Of course, we remained close with Grandma Edna. Bobby and I loved going to her house because there was a huge park across the street. He would push me on the merry-go-round, and we would always fight over the swing with the longer ropes. Grandma would yell across the road when it was time for lunch. She was the epitome of strength. Even though she was short in stature, she stood tall and proud. Her beautiful white, wavy hair was always perfectly pinned back with a broach comb on one side. In the back yard was a beautiful garden full of tomatoes, corn, and all types of fresh herbs. Bobby and I would spend all day picking vegetables and playing with the worms. After a long day outside, we would sit out under the big tree in the front yard with the freshly picked tomatoes and eat them like apples with a sprinkle of salt. If you are from Arkansas, you know there is nothing better!

Grandma Edna was married, but even when I was young, I could tell she didn't like him very much. She was always yelling at him and nagging at him for something as if he was a child. It often seemed as if there were dark secrets entangling my family and even though they tried to shield me from it, I knew things weren't completely right. I have memories of a man living behind her house who just got out of prison and I went to visit him one time and Grandma came in there screaming at me to not go back over there again. But in the midst of all this, there was one glimmer of light coming from out back of Grandma Edna's. Inside a little run down guest house in the backyard, which was more of a shack, lived Granny. Granny was Edna's mom, and my great-great-grandmother. She had the sweetest spirit and exuded love and peace. There was something different about her than most people I was around. Something refreshing. Something reassuring. A quiet strength that I didn't think could exist in such a dark world. I so badly wanted what she had. I wanted her kind of peace.

I know I speak about Grandma Edna as if she was my grandmother rather than my great-grandmother, and that is because my grandmother Bonnie (mom's mom), was not around as much. She actually began the cycle of abandonment when she left my mom to be raised by Grandma Edna. Sometimes during the summer, we would go visit her and Papaw in Okalona, Arkansas. We did enjoy visiting them. Bonnie always had something good cooking, but my favorite was her fried potatoes and pinto beans. She would let me play with makeup and when I wasn't too busy braiding her hair, Bobby and I would run wild on the four wheelers. No matter what we were doing, one thing was always true: Grandma Bonnie loved her beer and she was never without one.

We had lots of laughs and love, despite the dysfunction, but there was just always something missing for me everywhere I went.

I was just a few years old when my dad met his second wife. She and her two daughters moved in and I felt like I was in heaven. I had sisters and a mom; it started to feel like a family again. We became so close and they treated me as if I was their real sister. They even let me tag along when they went to visit their grandma and grandpa. One trip, we all went as a family to celebrate their grandpa's birthday. It seemed like the whole neighborhood was over. The men were huddled around a grill and the women were chasing kids and setting the table. My step-sisters and I were running around chasing lightning bugs on bicycles when we heard my dad yell, "Get away from that mud puddle." Dad, although stern, was a bit of a softie. We giggled a bit, but kept playing. Before long, we were all covered in mud. They called us up to the house and made us strip down to be hosed off before entering the house. Even at four years old, I was completely ashamed as I walked through the crowded porch up to the house. Feelings of guilt and humiliation consumed me, not only in that moment but for years to come. I stuffed the shame down as far as I could and always pretended to be strong and brave, even though on the inside I was broken and afraid.

Three

IT'S ALL MY FAULT
PART I

You know, the encyclopedia talks about how preschoolers handle abandonment. "Preschoolers tend to have a limited and mistaken perception of abandonment. They are highly self-centered with a strict sense of right and wrong. So when bad things happen to them, they usually blame themselves by assuming they did something wrong. Children this age often interpret the departure of a parent as a personal rejection."[2] This was most definitely me.

At five years old, right before starting kindergarten, my stepmom divorced my dad, which meant that my new family that I had come to love so much was gone. I had lived through so much hurt and internal pain already in just a short 5 years. Abandoned, rejected, lonely, unsettled, and unwanted. Worthless. I was already carrying so much baggage at such a young age. And I took the blame for it all, just like the encyclopedia said a preschooler does.

How could they leave us? This is all my fault. No one wants to be around me. What did I do wrong? Am I not good enough? Do I cause them too much stress? Do I not listen well enough? Am I too dumb for anyone to love me?

These were the thoughts that the voices in my head had been whispering. Only now, they weren't whispering, but almost yelling. I knew it had to be my fault. First, my mom left us, and now my stepmom and sisters. My dad did his best to recover, but another piece of his heart had been stolen and the only way he knew how to cope was to ignore it, stuff it as far down as possible, and pretend as if it never happened. The result was that my dad became even more distant and more closed off.

[2]Gale, Thomson. "Abandonment." Gale Encyclopedia of Children's Health: Infancy through Adolescence. Detroit: Gale, 2011. Encyclopedia.com. Web. 23 Dec. 2017.

I remember my first day of kindergarten. I was so nervous to leave my dad. But the yellow bus pulled up to get me as I was waiting at the bottom of our hill with my brother. It felt cold, and there were only strangers on the bus. We arrived at school and it was time to unload. Okay, but where do I go? Why are all of these other kids walking up with their parents? And then there was me, like I always was, alone. I finally got to my building and walked down the hall (which seemed a mile long). I found my classroom and I could feel the tears begin to well up in my eyes. I looked around searching for familiar faces but found none. I felt as if everyone was staring right at me wondering what I was doing there. It's simple; insecurity and fear were imbedded in me.

Though not without baggage or insecurities, I was making it through that year. I bet y'all are wondering where my mom was all this time, and the answer is, I didn't know. Just when things began to calm down, we were called to appear in court. I didn't understand most of the legal jargon that was being spoken, but at one point the judge called my name. "Jessica, do you know your mom?" I didn't even know why they were asking me this. I curled up next to Bobby and slouched down as far as I could. "Do you want to go stay with your mom?" This question I knew the answer to. I didn't want to be anywhere but with my dad. He was the only parent I knew. The only parent that was always there. I shouted, "No! I want to stay with my daddy!"

The judge continued to address my dad for what seemed like hours and by the end, we were ordered to spend the whole summer with her. She lived in a trailer park in Nashville, Arkansas with her husband and two sons. And again with the thoughts, *"Why am I being punished? Why couldn't she have stayed with her new family and left us alone?"*

I spent my last weeks of kindergarten just hoping it was all a bad dream. Surely, they were not going to force us to go in a live in a house with strangers. It was a long and quiet ride to meet Aunt Peggy. She was my dad's sister and was taking us the rest of the way to Nashville. Even though my dad was always quiet, this time the silence was unbearable. We arrived in the parking lot of an old feed store to meet Aunt Peggy. When we got in the car, she announced that she had a fun day planned. She was taking us to Magic Springs Theme Park. Bobby and I squealed as Dad loaded our bags into the car. We arrived at the park and for a moment, I almost forgot that we were soon to be in the house of a woman we did not know, with a family we had never met. We ran and played and had the best time riding every ride over and over. For the first time since we received the judge's order, I felt carefree. But the sun began to set, and the park was closing soon. Aunt Peggy called our names, "Bobby! Jessica! Time to go." Those words rang in my ears. My stomach sank. We headed to the car, drove out of the park, and were back on the road. I wondered what I could do to avoid this. *"Maybe I can jump out of the car and run away. Or maybe I can pretend I'm sick. Someone save me!"* Before I could make a move, we were turning on to the dark road of the trailer park. I was staring out the window at the trailers as we stopped in front of one. Aunt Peggy looked in the back seat at Bobby and I. "You two are going to be alright. Stick close to each other and always be there for each other. This summer will be over before you know it."

For some reason, the words meant to encourage did nothing but make me angry. I was beyond the point of tears. In fact, almost numb to sadness altogether. Now, I was just mad. My mom opened the front door and came outside. Although I still barely recognized her, as I only remembered seeing her a couple of times in my whole life. Behind her, I could see two boys peeking out along with a strange man. I knew this must be her new family. This was not my house or my family, this was a stranger's house. I was so angry. So on top of never feeling like I fit in, I am here watching my mom be a mom to this family. It often felt like an out-of-body experience; watching from the sidelines as this family went about their daily lives. None of it made sense and no one was talking about it.

I don't belong here. These people are not my family. I don't belong anywhere. Will I ever fit in?

I spent the summer resisting every bit of warmth she tried to give, and when it was finally over I was overjoyed to see Aunt Peggy as she arrived to pick us up. I ran out the front door, leaving my bags behind, and jumped into her arms. She picked me up and gave me a kiss on the forehead. It was the first gesture of love I had felt in months. She leaned down to pick up my bags and carried me to the car. I didn't want to let her go but I was just so excited to be going home. I missed my dad so much and couldn't wait to see him. Maybe he would hug me real big. He wasn't the hugging type and didn't say "I love you." But I know he loved me.

The ride home seemed longer than before, but Bobby and I were both more relaxed than we had been all summer. We finally pulled down the dirt road and I could see our house up on the hill. I wanted to jump out of the car right then and run up. As we pulled closer, I could see my dad outside, working on his old Ford truck. I couldn't keep from smiling. I jumped out of the car and ran as fast as I could to my dad. When he looked at me, I could tell these last couple of months hurt him. They created pain in his heart he hadn't felt before. I said, "I missed you so much, Daddy! Please don't ever let me go or make me go to her house again." He just smiled in his calm manner as if to reassure me, knowing he might not be able to prevent that if my mom continued to pursue visitation. We went inside and I sat in my favorite chair by the fireplace. I felt exhausted. After two months (which to a six year old feels like a year), I was finally able to relax. Dad was ready to "cook us dinner," which meant we jumped in his truck and headed to the Quick Stop to grab burgers and fresh fries. My dad tried cooking once and his burgers were as hard as a rock, so he didn't really try that anymore. We mostly had bologna sandwiches. When we got back I went to visit Grandpa across the field. I hoped things would just stay exactly like this, but unfortunately, it wouldn't last long.

With our stepmom and stepsisters gone, the house was quiet, but we had each other. Dad seemed to be working even harder these days, but when he was home, I was right by his side. I didn't play dressup or act very "girly." I would stand next to him as he worked on the old truck, handing him tools. I would talk his ear off about everything under the sun and he would listen quietly, sometimes responding with, "Mmhmm…"

I know he was smiling under that beard of his. I could always make him laugh. For a moment things were good, even when it was hard. That changed very quickly when my dad met his next wife, Kay. She was a high-class city girl, or a wannabe of sorts. She and her two kids moved in with us soon after they began dating. From the get-go, she was trying to change us. She made us go to church on Saturdays at a place where kids lived, went to school, and attended church. It was like a compound. We went from fried bologna sandwiches every day to vegetarian diets. She forced Bobby and me to take violin and piano lessons and she yelled at us when we made mistakes. And literally everything that went wrong somehow became my fault, even the time I got lice at school. I was sent home early, and when I got there, she looked at me as if I was the most repulsive thing she had ever seen. "It's your fault. You disgust me." What was worse was that Kay and my mom were out against each other. During a weekend visitation, my mom took me to get my ears pierced. As soon as I walked in the door, Kay ripped the earrings out of my ears.

I'm not good enough. I will never be good enough.

One day, she was yelling so much, I couldn't take it anymore. I ran out the door and over to Grandpa's. When I got there, already in tears, I couldn't find him. "Grandpa…. Grandpa!" No answer. He wasn't home. I walked outside and wondered where he was. I sat out on the porch for a few minutes until I saw my dad's truck driving up the hill to our house. He was finally home, only he was driving faster than normal. I ran over to meet him and he quickly told me to get in the truck. We left the house and began driving and I knew something was wrong. I looked up at him hoping for some sort of explanation, but he stayed silent. We drove for a while until we pulled in at the hospital in Hot Springs. I knew this couldn't be good. I mustered up all the strength I had, "Dad?" He looked at me and said, "It's your grandpa."

Those were the only words he said before we walked inside. My stomach was in knots and my mind was racing. I was a just an 8 year old little girl and I needed my grandpa. He, my dad, and Bobby were all I had. I was instructed to sit out in the hall while Dad went into his hospital room. What seemed like hours later, Dad came out of the room in tears. I had never seen Dad cry before and it did something to me. I felt my heart crumbling into pieces. He was gone. After this, Dad's marriage to Kay took a turn for the worse and she went away with her son and daughter. First, my mom, then two stepmoms and all of my step-brothers and sisters, then my grandpa. In eight years, I had already experienced more loss than some people do in their whole lives. And each time, the same feelings of abandonment took over. I was suddenly back in that infant car seat, on the front porch with a note taped to me. "I can't do this anymore."

As abandonment swirled around my life, I was trying to fit into elementary school and it was a nightmare. I hated school and correction from the teachers. I didn't have popular things like other kids and I was be made fun of for what I was wearing. One of the worst days was the day I came to school with my new little boy haircut. I remember being on the swings and kids coming around me, laughing and pointing. If only they knew the hurt I had been through they may have been more kind.

PART II

Revisiting these stories and reliving them as I write this book is difficult. To this day, I still want to be loved and wanted. Still today, I wish I had a normal childhood and felt loved. However, that isn't my story and probably is not your story either. So, how would I ever overcome these abandonment issues? Spoiler alert! I gave my life to Christ, but that doesn't take away the pain or make my life a "happily ever after" story, just like that. I had to let God go in and strip away all of the lies that I believed. I had to learn His truth about what He says about me. Frankly, that is the reason this book has been such a pain in my butt to write. I have a story that is full of hurt, then I have a whole other life that I have lived that tells of the Truth that would set me free. So, I want to share with you the wisdom and truth I have learned that helped me out of my prison. This information addresses the root of the problem, rather than the surface.

First, you have to know that when someone walks out on your life, it is never your fault. Even if they say it is, it is never your fault. There is something else, much bigger, going on inside of that person that you don't know and may never be told. More than anything, I wish someone would have shared this truth with me, and I actually would have believed it. I wish I would have known my mother was fighting internal demons and that there was a power that could save her so she would have stayed. Also, death was such a hard thing for me to get over because I didn't understand why we were born to live and then die. As a child, your mind can't process this in a healthy way if you have no one to explain the pain to you and help you walk through it. All of it begins to pile up inside, one on top of the other, until you explode and begin to make one bad decision after another. That is what happened to me. I went into a downward spiral and couldn't grab ahold of anything that would save me from hitting the pavement. I kept screaming for help, but no one around me had ever climbed out of their own darkness to help me manage mine. So, dysfunction kept raising dysfunction.

When you have been abandoned and you believe you are the reason you were abandoned, you actually start abandoning yourself. We start to live out what we have felt the world was showing us. We have a fear that everyone else that comes into our lives will do the same thing. The real and raw truth is that this thinking actually creates our actions; people don't want to be around us, so they end up leaving like we knew they would. It is our own walls and defense tactics that hurt us the most. When we stop loving ourselves, we create an atmosphere for no one else to show us true, healthy love. The baggage you carry from what your past has done to you will ruin your future! We have to get in God's word and let him heal us. Also, consider counseling. Find someone to help you walk through the true root of all your issues. If you have been abandoned, I would bet that you can trace most of your issues back to that. You see, the enemy uses our pain to make us doubt God's goodness, but His word can pierce through that and speak straight to our hearts. These scriptures gave me a quiet revelation that proved He was there the whole time.

Psalm 27:10 NLT- Even if my father and my mother abandoned me, the Lord will hold me close.

Deuteronomy 31:6 NLT- So be strong and courageous! Do not be afraid and do not panic before them. For the Lord your God will personally go ahead of you. He will neither fail you nor abandon you.

2 Corinthians 4:8-9 NLT- We are pressed on every side by troubles, but we are not crushed. We are perplexed, but not driven to despair. We are hunted down, but never abandoned by God. We get knocked down, but we are not destroyed.

Mark 15:34 NLT- Then at three o'clock Jesus cried with a loud voice, "Eloi, Eloi, lema sabachthani?" which means, "My God, My God, why have You abandoned me?"

See how relatable these truth bombs are?! If we actually believe that He wants to hold us close and that He will never leave us, it will save us a lot of pain. So, with these scriptures and if God's word is the same yesterday, today, and forever (which the Bible says it is), then you and I can walk in this freedom. Despite the cards you or I were dealt, He has a plan and a purpose for our lives.

Four

REJECTION
PART I

The feeling of abandonment leads to rejection. It is possible to experience post-traumatic stress syndrome from being abandoned. To be honest, I believe this is what happened to me. All of the trauma surrounding my life: my mom leaving, but not just her, also the step-moms that came and went. All of those experiences are considered abandonment, but this developed a feeling of rejection inside of me. I thought they didn't want to be around me and that maybe I was too bad for them to accept. I had those, "no one is ever going to love me" kind of thoughts. So, moving forward in this chapter, I am going to take you through what I call my "middle school hell years." I am sure you have those years on some level, too.

Since having PTSD from the abandonment, I felt as though every situation was a big deal and it always sent my emotions into a downward spiral. Like, if someone made a rude comment, pointed and laughed, or if I was picked last, I would lose complete control of my emotions. As we southerners say, "I would flip my lid," and it would take over my life in that moment. Then, that moment of hurt would be put into my box of "things Jessica has done wrong" and it would be marked as one more reason I was a loser. I would replay my past over and over when the smallest of things would happen. My mood was dependent on how I expected everyone to treat me, and we all know that in middle school no one treats anyone nicely. So my hurt was confirmed over and over. I felt that I was not worthy of love and that this world would constantly reject me. The bottom line is: my childhood trauma would play a part in how I filtered my life. Everything was rooted in insecurity. I mean, if my own mom didn't want me what was I worth to this life? Why was I even born? Rejection is like a broken record; it plays over and over in the back of your mind. With these thoughts, my self-esteem went to crap (for lack of a better word), and I became a walking time bomb of emotions.

If you have been abandoned or rejected, you have probably noticed a ripple effect of these emotions that trickled into other areas of your life. For example, these are just a few (seriously there were too many to count), of the battles I faced heading into middle school:

1. Extreme sensitivity to peers.
2. Needing acceptance and validation.
3. Self-destructive/suicide attempts
4. Issues with authority figures
5. Isolation

Elementary school had been difficult, but nothing prepared me for what I was about to endure. I had hoped that entering middle school might mean a fresh start. Maybe I could find something I was good at. During the first week of school, I walked the halls with my head down hoping to just be invisible. I sat alone in the lunch room until one day another girl came up to my table. I heard, "Is someone sitting here?"

"Um, uhh, no. No one is sitting there." I was in shock that someone was talking to me, much less sitting at the lunch table with me. I continued eating my cafeteria lunch, (which was terrible, but I was hungry). My new table mate must've known, because she offered me her graham crackers. I gratefully accepted. She had a friendly smile and was heavyset. But I didn't care.

"My name is Jessica."

"I'm Dana."

And just like that, I had a new friend. We sat together every day after that and within a couple of weeks, she had invited me to spend the night at her house. I was thrilled to be doing something that every other kid my age was doing. That Thursday night, I stayed up late packing my bag to take to school on Friday to stay at Dana's house.

I felt so grown up walking into school that morning. I had a friend. And I, Jessica Teague, was going to a sleepover. The day couldn't pass fast enough before the bell finally rang. I rushed out of the classroom and into to hall towards Dana's locker. I had the biggest smile on my face as I walked quickly, trying to restrain myself from running. I didn't want to risk seeming uncool. I finally spotted Dana standing with some other girls.

"Are y'all ready?" Dana asked. Y'all? Who does she mean? I thought Dana had just invited me over. To my surprise, there were two other girls coming with us. These other girls weren't like me. One of them had shoulder length blond hair perfectly curled and a pretty bright pink dress. The other was still in her basketball clothes, but her hair was in a perfect ponytail and I noticed her brand new Nike tennis shoes. I knew I didn't fit in with these girls. I suddenly felt my stomach sink and wanted nothing else but to walk the other way. But it was too late.

"Umm, yes," I stuttered.

"Yes, we are ready! Let's go play beauty shop!"

Dana led the way to her mom's car. She said, "My mom is making cookies for us and we are going to order pizza." Part of me was so excited to be experiencing so many firsts. The other part of me felt like I shouldn't even be here. What did I have in common with these girls? We arrived at Dana's house and my nerves had calmed some. Her mother, Mrs. Allen, was so warm and welcoming. The house was so neat and tidy and smelled like flowers and freshly baked cookies. Is this real life? This must be what it's like to have a mom around all the time.

We scarfed down our pizza and then went into Dana's room to change into our pajamas. Of course, mine were just an old pair of sweats and one of Bobby's oversized t-shirts. I pretended not to notice that they were all in matching pink plaid pajamas straight off of a Dillard's mannequin. We were sitting around Dana's room when one of the girls pulled out a bag of makeup. Real makeup. Grownup makeup. "Time for makeovers!"

I had played with makeup at my grandma Bonnie's but I had never worn it myself. I didn't even know how to ask Dad for makeup, and even if I did, we didn't have money for fancy things like that. All the girls were shuffling through the compacts and lipsticks. I just sat there, staring. Dana opened up some eye shadow and started applying it as if she were a professional. The other girls were applying lipstick. "Jessica, don't you want to try some?"

"I... umm... I've never worn makeup before." I was scared to admit it but I couldn't fake my way through this one.

"What do you mean? Haven't you played with your mom's?" The girls looked at each other and giggled as if I weren't in the room.

"It's ok, Jessica! Let me give you a makeover," Dana gave me a reassuring smile and the girls a warning glare. I felt a slight bit of dignity return when she stood up for me. I sat there on the edge of the bed while she dusted my face with objects I had never seen. Telling me when to open and close my eyes, when to open my mouth, and when to rub my lips together. Though it felt quite different than times spent with my dad in the shop helping rebuild motors, I loved it. I looked in the mirror and didn't recognize myself. For a minute, I felt like I could be pretty. Of course, it never fails, the thoughts were back. "Who am I kidding? I will never be like the other girls."

The next morning, I woke up to the smell of bacon and pancakes. I looked around to see that all the other girls were still sound asleep. My stomach was rumbling and I didn't want to wake them so I quietly climbed out of the bed and walked into the dining room. Mrs. Allen was setting the table and humming softly as I caught her eye.

"Good morning, pretty girl," she said as she motioned me over to the table. I looked behind me to make sure she was talking to me. I sat down at the table and my eyes widened at the ginormous breakfast spread. Bacon, pancakes, eggs, fried potatoes, and a bowl of fresh fruit. Everything was displayed neatly on platters and almost looked too pretty to eat. Almost.

"Help yourself to whatever you would like, Jessica." Although we didn't have fancy things, my dad always taught me to be polite and respectful. I grabbed a little of everything and waited while she poured me a glass of milk. It was delicious and I savored every bite. By the time I was finished, the other girls were up and at the table. We talked about the night before and all of the girly activities. It had been fun, but there was still a cloud hanging over me. I knew I didn't fit in with these girls, but I was determined to try.

After breakfast, I went into the room to pack my things before my dad arrived to pick me up. I could hear the other girls giggling and whispering in the living room as I walked back in. One of the girls pointed out the window and asked, "Is that your ride?" I could feel my face get hot as I pulled my bag closer to me for comfort. My dad was outside in his old beat up Thunderbird.

"Yes. That's my daddy." The girls were trying to stifle their giggles as Mrs. Allen hushed them. I walked toward the door in complete embarrassment. I thanked Mrs. Allen for having me and walked out quickly to keep from crying. I could feel them watching out the window in ridicule and maybe even pity. My dad, being a man of few words, didn't ask any questions although I'm sure he knew something was wrong. I didn't want him to see me cry. It wasn't his fault that my mom left. It wasn't his fault that money was tight. He worked so hard to give us everything we needed. I stayed quiet and decided to shove the feelings down and get back to my reality. I was glad to be home with Dad and Bobby.

The next week at school, Dana and I went back to our typical lunch routine at the table in the far back corner. The other girls from the sleepover sat at a table across the cafeteria with the popular group. I was starting to realize that Dana was just as much of an outcast as I was and that hosting the sleepover did not quite win her a seat at the cool kids table. I was just grateful to have an escape from class. Elementary school was a challenge, but now in middle school, I was struggling in every subject. I didn't comprehend math equations or retain historical facts. I wasn't a very good reader and spelling was not my strong suit. I tried to focus, but as the days went on, the more lost I felt. Dad did his best to help me with homework, but he was busy trying to provide for us and I was left to my own devices.

One day in Mrs. Turner's science class, she announced that we were starting a new project. Our project could be based on a scientific experiment or career exploration in a field that we were interested in pursuing in the future. I had no interest in science. In fact, I could barely read half the words in our textbook, so I decided I would choose a career. Since the sleepover, I had been thinking about how it felt to feel pretty, even if only for a moment. It was then that the idea of helping make others feel pretty was sparked inside me. "Hair stylist!" I shouted out by accident.

"That sounds great, Jessica," Mrs. Turner smiled sweetly at me as if she knew my motives. I was excited to begin working on my project to present to the class at the end of the semester. I sat through the remainder of the class daydreaming about my future. This was it! This was what I wanted to be when I grew up. I couldn't wait to tell Dana at lunch.

As I made my way to my lunch table, I saw the girls from the sleepover across the room. I was still embarrassed from the ridicule of the sleepover and kept my head down to avoid eye contact. I spotted Dana walk up to their table and I could tell she was hoping they would invite her to stay. As she walked away, I watched as the girls begin to whisper and point. They continued giggling and staring as she made her way to our table. I thought, "Maybe they don't like her because she's my friend. Or maybe they don't like me because I'm her friend."

The weeks went on and I had distanced myself from Dana. I was desperate to be part of the popular group and I thought if I could join them in their bullying, I might gain their approval. One day in P.E, I started making fun of her with the other kids. I walked over and pushed her. Dana looked at me in shock and shoved me back. We were suddenly cat fighting for a solid minute before the coach came up and pulled us apart. He marched us straight to the principal's office and as we were walking away, I looked back in pride hoping to see the other kids cheering me on. Instead, they were laughing hysterically and pointing at both of us. What had I done? Guilt and shame seeped into my pores and I immediately felt the sting of more rejection. I had ruined my friendship with my only true friend and dug myself into a deeper pit of isolation.

After two days of suspension from the fight, I dreaded walking back in to P.E. class to be criticized and ridiculed. The coach announced that we were playing kickball and two captains were nominated to choose their teams. One by one, each of the other kids were called until finally only Dana and I were left. To my misery, her name was called and I was standing alone as the coach motioned for me to join the second team. As I was walking over a fly landed on my face. "Disgusting! She attracts flies. We don't want her on our team," one of the boys yelled.

I was completely humiliated. The other kids joined in on the laughter as the coach hushed them up and told us to get in place. With my head down, I walked to the back of the field, just hoping the ball wouldn't come my way. The voices in my head couldn't be silenced. I spent the rest of that year laying low and staying as far away from everyone as I could. I had been hurt so much in my life by people and their actions. I knew I had to be the problem.

Disgusting. Ugly. Stupid. Loser. No one likes me. I shouldn't even be here!

The remaining weeks of middle school were long and dreadful. Every day I felt myself dodging another bully's hurtful antics. It had become my norm and I felt alone and forgotten. I think most of the teachers knew, but most of them seemed to look the other way. I had no one to come to my defense.

There was one boy who was nice to me even when his friends weren't. His name was Eric. And although he wasn't very cute, I was desperate for anyone to accept me. He would smile at me when he saw me in the hall, and I smiled back. It was the only interaction I had to look forward to. One day in the cafeteria, Eric came and sat across from me. I looked around thinking maybe he had made a mistake and sat at the wrong table.

"Hi, Jessica… I just wanted to tell you, I think you are really pretty… and I wanted to ask you if you would be my girlfriend." He finally looked up from his hands as he finished the sentence and he smiled shyly. I felt my jaw drop and my eyes were as wide as they could get. Thoughts were flooding my mind as I stuttered to answer.

This must be a joke. There is no way he likes me. His friends are probably waiting around the corner to yell "Gotcha!"

I was silent for at least a whole minute until finally I decided that a chance at acceptance was worth the risk of being ridiculed if it were a joke. "Umm… yes, I will. I will be your girlfriend."

"Good," he said with a smile of relief, "So, what do we do now?"

I had never had a boyfriend but lots of the other kids at school were coupling up. Of course, that pretty much just entailed sitting together at lunch, and hanging out in P.E. I was going to be the best girlfriend ever and I wanted everyone to know that I had a boyfriend. "Well, there's movie day coming up next week. We could sit together and, um, hold hands." I held my breath a little bit, nervous of how he would respond to my bright idea.

"I've never held hands before," he said with a bit of reluctance.

"Me either, but we could try."

"Ok, it's a deal. Movie day. I'll save you a seat." He seemed to be growing fond of the idea by the end of the conversation. I was nervous but confident. Maybe once people see that I had a boyfriend, they would accept me. If not, at least I had Eric.

Word travels fast in a small school and by lunch the next day, people were already talking about our plan. Each day the buzz grew louder and by movie day, the whole school was talking about it. I walked into the gym, proud and excited, and spotted Eric as he waved me over. I sat down and nerves set in. How was this going to happen? Was he going to grab my hand or was I going to grab his? I was sitting on his right with my left hand sitting on my leg, openly available for the taking. The movie finally started and the lights were dimmed, but still bright enough for everyone around us to spectate this big event. Our hands slowly crept closer and closer until finally, they touched and boom! Our hands were locked and I was beaming with pride until suddenly, everyone began laughing hysterically. What did I do wrong? We were just holding hands. Is there even a wrong way to hold hands?

In that very moment, my heart sank, my stomach knotted up, and I felt a wave of pure humiliation consume my entire body. Everything around me disappeared and I was suddenly frozen with fear as the voices in my head screamed louder than ever before.

Nobody likes you! Your mom didn't love you! You are worthless, useless, and you will never be good enough!

I ran to the bathroom and stayed there for the rest of the day until the bell rang. I was the first one out the door before anyone could see me. I went straight to the bus and hurried to the very back row and ducked down in the seat as far as I could. I was on the verge of tears but was determined not to let any of those mean kids see me cry. The driver finally stopped in front of my house and I grabbed and things and walked quickly down the aisle. Kids were giggling and I could hear the names they were calling me.

I rushed into the house and dropped to my knees in tears. I couldn't stand the pain. I was just twelve years old, but I didn't want to live anymore. I ran in the kitchen and grabbed a knife out of the drawer. I wanted this all to end. The pain... the heartache... the rejection. I couldn't take it anymore. I thought if the knife would go through my heart the pain I felt would end, so I kept the knife with me as I walked into my room. I heard my dad come in the front door and I quickly put it under my pillow. I didn't want my dad to see me like this. He wasn't good with emotions. He had seen me cry many days after school, and although I know it hurt his heart to watch, he didn't know how to help me.

I cried so hard that my head was throbbing and my eyes were sore. But, as I laid in bed that night, wondering how I was going to make it through, something deep inside kept telling me to keep on going. Just one more day. One more day to make it through, and in ten years, none of this will matter. Things can't possibly get any worse, so surely that means it will only get better. So, I kept on for another day. And another.

PART II

Do you ever ask yourself, "What if I would have known about this or that?" What if I had been shown how to deal with all of this rejection? Would I still have gone into a downward spiral? I can't answer that, and neither can you. What I know now is that you don't have to go down the wrong path just because you were born into a dysfunctional life.

We are going to face battles and we are going to be rejected by people. That is because people are fickle and imperfect human beings. That is literally called LIFE. But, we can't take someone else's insecurities and wear them as our own. You never know what someone is dealing with. Maybe they are experiencing PTSD. Maybe they just had a bad day. Maybe they are being abused every single night. Whatever it is, we can't depend on people to show us our worth and value. I guarantee that it will leave you feeling rejected in some form, every single time.

So what does God's Word have to say about how we handle rejection?

Psalm 34:17-20 NIV- The righteous cry out, and the Lord hears them; He delivers them from all their troubles. The Lord is close to the brokenhearted and saves those who are crushed in spirit. The righteous person may have many troubles, but the Lord delivers him from them all. He protects all of his bones, not one of them will be broken.

John 15:18-19 NIV- "If the world hates you, keep in mind that it hated me first. If you belonged to the world, it would love you as its own. As it is, you do not belong to the world, but I have chosen you out of the world. That is why the world hates you."

1 Peter 2:4-6 NIV- As you come to him, the living Stone- rejected by humans, but chosen by God and precious to Him. You also, like living stones, are being built into a spiritual house to be a holy priesthood, offering spiritual sacrifices acceptable to God through Jesus Christ. For in Scripture it says: See, I lay a stone in Zion, a chosen and precious cornerstone, and the one who trusts Him, will never be put to shame.

I am amazed every time I read the Bible because it always feels like it is speaking directly into my heart and the battle that I might be facing. Another important piece to this puzzle is worship. There are songs that are written when in suffering and they will speak directly to my heart as well. I encourage you to listen to and download worship music. For ones that speak directly to rejection, download: "Words" by Hawk Nelson and "Even If" by MercyMe. Let the words wash over your soul. Let them shine a light into your darkness.

Five

ADDICTION

ad·dic·tion

The state of being enslaved to a habit or practice or to something that is psychologically or physically habitforming, such as narcotics, to such an extent that its cessation causes severe trauma.[3]

Just like abandonment leads to rejection, rejection leads to addiction. *At least pornography, alcohol, drugs, and other addictions can't leave me. I can control these things.* How funny is it that we think we can control addiction?

"Enslaved" is a great word to describe the world of addiction. It takes total control over your life and mind. It's all you care about. It's your go-to if someone hurts you or rejects you. The definition even says stopping this addiction can cause severe trauma, but staying enslaved to it can be so much worse. The problem is, you can't see how it's ruining your life. You think it's all fun and games at first. The rush is like no other. The excitement of this new found thing overtakes your thoughts. Then it controls your actions. Then you fall into the guilt cycle of letting something have that much control over you, so you just do it again. This horrible cycle continues over and over until, as you've heard it, you've "hit rock bottom." Everyone's rock bottom looks different. This particular story is not yet my rock bottom, but I did get there. So, what took control of my life first? A guy. Yep, you read that right, a guy. The sad thing is, this is not talked about a lot in the realm of women. That is why, even more so, I want to share it with you. I want to reiterate that you're not alone. Get help. Let the shame stop haunting you.

After barely surviving fifth grade, I was relieved and excited for summer. No

[3]dictionary.com

bullies, no homework, and plenty of time to spend helping Dad in the shop. One night, one of my dad's friends stopped by to drop something off. It was a VHS movie. I was so excited and wanted so badly to watch it. My dad, being the man he was, ordered me to my room and told me that the movie was an adult movie only.

What did he mean this movie was for adults only? I was twelve and I had already seen other Rated R movies. I obeyed my dad, but the curiosity was taking me over. I waited until the next day when everyone was gone and I was home alone. I went into the living room to search for the movie. My dad had hidden it back behind the TV in an effort to keep me from finding it. Good try, Dad.

Within minutes, there were images on the screen that I had never seen before. Men and women, naked, doing things that I had never even imagined. In an instant, my innocence was stolen. I was now an even more curious pre-teenaged girl who knew far more than any young girl should. I had feelings of guilt as the movie played, but also feelings of excitement, as I knew I wanted to see it all again. The next day, I found myself home alone again. I felt a rush as I went back to the secret hiding spot to grab the movie and start over. My heart was racing because I was nervous that I'd get caught, but also because I was excited to learn more of what love was. I was addicted to this feeling! I felt the rush through my whole body, but didn't understand why it made me feel this way. It was a rush, an escape from my own misery. I couldn't wait to be home alone again.

One day my closest neighbor was moving out and new neighbors were moving in. I stopped by one day to say "hi," and I saw they had a daughter a few years older than me. She was tall and pretty and had a warm smile under her perfectly glossed lips. I had been alone most of the summer, so I was glad to be out of the house and to be interacting with someone other than my family.

"I'm Karen. We just moved here from Oklahoma."

"It's a small town and once school starts you'll know everyone there is to know within a week." She laughed at my joke and I was pleased with my own ice breaker.

"Do you want to come over to my house and hang out? We could watch TV or listen to music." I knew I should probably wait until Dad got home to ask for permission, but I was feeling more grown up now and decided I could make my own decision. I could tell she was older than me and I didn't want to seem like a baby.

"Sure, that sounds fun." We walked together down the road to Karen's house and went in to her room. There were still boxes around but she had lots of girly things, like a matching bed spread and pillow cases, and pictures on the walls. It felt cozy and I loved it. I walked around her room looking at all the pictures she had with her friends. There were several cute boys and I couldn't help but notice Karen being quite close to them in some pictures. If only Karen knew that I was the loser of Kirby Middle School, she might not want to hang out with me anymore. I wanted to be just like her when I was her age. She was fifteen and had started to develop, and it was obvious that she knew how to attract attention.

Karen and I spent almost every day together just laughing, talking, and doing what teenage girls do. I looked up to her like a sister and we told each other everything. One day she grabbed her journal and flipped through the pages until she got to a list of boys' names. She gave me a mischievous smile and handed it to me to look at.

"What is this?" I asked with the little bit of innocence I had left.

"It's my list, silly! Every guy I have messed around with. You know, like make out sessions, second base, sex. I like to keep track of them," she said without hesitation. I gasped with amusement, knowing that this was wrong but it felt so right. I wanted to have my own list like Karen. I had seen these things done in the movie, but I had never thought of doing them myself. She told me all about her experiences with guys in detail and I was in shock and awe at the same time. She introduced me to masturbation, and this became something I struggled with for years along with the pornography. It created more shame and hopelessness and I thought, "Surely, I'm not the only one with this secret?

I know how uncomfortable you might feel right now, but trust me, it is really embarrassing being the one writing it twenty-five years later. The reason I am choosing to write this is because you wouldn't believe how many girls are trapped in this lifestyle and feel like they are the only ones in it.

That summer was truly the end of my innocence. I couldn't wait to start seventh grade with my newfound knowledge. Karen taught me how to dress sexier and wear makeup, and sometimes she would sneak some of her dad's whiskey for us. I went into the school year with more confidence than ever before. Boys were noticing me and I was getting good at flirting. After the first week of school, everyone planned to hang out at the skating rink. I went over to Karen's to get ready and her mom gave us a ride into town. I quickly spotted my newest crush. I didn't know his name, but I was determined to have my first kiss that night. With all that I had seen in the movie, I knew I would be a pro. I eyed him down for a while until he finally noticed. He came over to me and grabbed my hand and led me out onto the rink. We skated around for a couple of songs until finally a slow song came on. I pulled him over to the side and laid one on him. I think he was in shock but he didn't stop. We kissed for a good two minutes before finally someone came over and told us to break it up. I loved the feeling of being wanted, and learning how to entice and control men made me feel temporarily accepted. Although when I was in bed at night, alone with my addiction, guilt and shame hung over my head like a dark cloud.

Every weekend we would go to the skating rink, and I would roam the rink until I found the cutest boy there and do it all over again. After a while, making out wasn't enough. I wanted more. One Friday night, a group of older guys were hanging out at the rink and I knew this was my chance to graduate from amateur make out sessions to the big leagues. There was one guy staring at me from across the room and my heart raced with excitement as he approached me.

"I just wanted you to know, I saw you from across the room and I couldn't take my eyes off you. My name is Devin, by the way. Can I take you out sometime?"

"How about tomorrow? I'll meet you here at 7:00," I said with flirtatious confidence.

"It's a date, beautiful." I could feel myself blushing as he walked away. He didn't even ask for my name, but he could call me beautiful any time he wanted. We met up the next night and he took me to the local restaurant. For once, I felt desired as he showered me with compliments. We continued hanging out every weekend and eventually he asked me to be his girlfriend. He was much older than me, so I had to keep it a secret, but I didn't care. It was almost my thirteenth birthday and I decided I was ready to give him more but not all. There was a big party happening in the next town over and I told my dad I was staying the night at Karen's so we could stay out all night. We got ready at Karen's and then snuck out after her parents were asleep. Devin and his friends picked us up and we headed to the party. I had a couple of beers on the way and the next thing I knew, I woke up in a bedroom that I had never seen before. I didn't remember making it to the party or anything that happened. Was I drugged? Did I drink more than I thought?

My head was pounding and my hands were shaking. I scrambled to gather my things and find Karen. I went into the living room and found her passed out on the couch along with several other people I had never seen. I woke her up and we offered every dollar that we had (which wasn't much) to a guy who would drive us home. When we pulled into the driveway, Dad was standing there waiting with Karen's dad. I knew this wasn't good, but I didn't care. We got out of the car and Karen went straight into her house with her dad and I followed mine home. That road had never seemed so long. Dad was silent as usual but he didn't have to say a word. I felt disgusting and dirty and full of shame. I wasn't even sure what had happened but it was enough to make me feel an inch tall. I wanted to crawl in bed and never wake up.

A few weeks after that night, Devin broke up with me. During this break-up I was going to see my mom some, and she ended up being pregnant for the fifth time. Being thirteen now, I actually got really excited. I was going to have a baby sister. Something I had always dreamed about. But my relationship with my mom was based on her mood or what was going on in her world. She had me around during her pregnancy for visitations, but that changed when she went into the hospital to have the baby girl. She told my step dad to take me home; that she didn't want me being around this baby and teaching this new baby my bad ways. She wanted this one to turn out right. *Turn out right?* Like I was all of the wrong things. The emotions fled back. Abandoned, rejected, unwanted, unloved. I was hurt all over again, so I threw myself onto boys even harder. They were my source for temporary pain relief. It was in this season that I met Sam.

Sam showed me a love I had never felt. He told me everything I wanted to hear. He would show up with a Dr. Pepper and a Snickers just to show me he cared. His friend would tell me how hard Sam had fallen for me and that I was his one and only. I felt this was special; it was different than what I had with Devin. So, I planned out how I would lose my virginity to him. I wanted to give him my all so he would stay with me forever. In my plan, I needed to get away for a whole weekend. I told my dad I was going to stay with my mom. But, we all know that I didn't make it to my mom's house; I made it to Sam's house. We had the best time that weekend. We went hunting and drove around backroads listening to music. It was like a scene from your typical country music song. I was sitting right next to my happily ever after, my dream guy. The way he looked at me made me melt. And then that November night came. I had just turned fifteen. I was a little girl who thought she was grown. I thought I was old enough to be making these decisions. I thought I was fully prepared to take this next step. So, I did. Just like that, we made "magical" love for all of five minutes. It was not like I saw in the movies. He passed out and I was lying there with tears streaming down my face and regret was the song playing in my head. Can I have a do-over? Can I undo what I just did?

Finally, I dozed off to sleep only to be awakened by a loud knock on his bedroom door and screaming from a woman. Was this his mother? Who was this? I opened the door and there stood a beautiful woman who was nine months pregnant. She was hysterical. What just happened?! I gave him my all and it was based on a lie? Another person that claimed to love me and never leave me was never even mine. He had a family he was dedicated to. So then why did he want me? For his own pleasure? To rip my heart out of my chest? Well, ladies and gentlemen, he got what he wanted. I went home after my encounter with his "baby momma" and never talked to him again. The pain was strong and so real. I said in the weeks after this that I would never let anyone hurt me again. No one would ever have my full emotions. No one was ever going to play Jessica Teague again. I was going to be in control, so that I could play and hurt everyone else. I became very promiscuous, seeking attention from any man that would look my way. Parties and sneaking out became a regular part of my routine, and it seemed as if each time I drank more, went further, pushed the envelope just a little more than the time before. I was desperate for something to fill the huge black hole inside my heart, but the excitement and pleasure were only temporary. Waking up the morning after a binge, I would feel the claws of regret sinking into my soul, each time a little deeper. More shame, more guilt, more inadequacy. Something inside of me knew this wasn't the right way to live, and that there had to be more. I would promise myself to be better, to change, but the temptation was just too much. And I would cry every time, hoping for someone to save me from this misery.

Six
EMPTINESS
PART I

emp·ti·ness

The feeling, or rather the lack of it, that one wishes to fulfill, but can never seem to get right.[4]

Addiction leaves you empty and searching for more. I would say there is no emptier feeling than when you give your virginity to someone outside of marriage. You may not have had as dramatic of an experience as I did my first time, but even so, you probably sat there naked, feeling empty, hollow, worthless, angry, and sad, all wrapped into one. I have even known girls who have struggled with depression and body images issues after losing their virginity. I didn't even grow up in a Christian household, but I still knew that I shouldn't have had sex before marriage. It was just one more thing to add to the long list of baggage. Metaphorically speaking, at this point, it looked like I was packing up and moving out with all of the bags I was carrying.

Junior high was finally here, and that summer I had found a cool groove. Middle school was but a distant memory and I was determined to maintain my new found "cool girl" reputation. I finally found a sense of belonging on the basketball team. I had played in middle school and was naturally athletic. Basketball was the only thing I had to look forward to where school was concerned. It was the only thing I felt like I was good at, even though I was constantly selfcriticizing, and my coach would yell at me and take me out of games when I messed up. I just wanted to be good enough at one thing in my life.

By this time, I had mastered the art of gaining male attention and I continued to seek it. People had told me my whole life that I was beautiful, and even though I felt ugly, I was going to use this attention to my benefit. The rush I felt when I could walk past a guy and get him to look my direction temporarily bandaged my longing for love and acceptance. I could gain any guy's attention, but once he got what he wanted from me, I was left alone again. The hole in my heart had grown so big, but I had become used to the pain. It was a part of me.

Jennifer and I grew inseparable. She was the only person that understood me. We had known each other since we were in middle school, but had grown closer over the last couple of years while playing basketball together. We were like two peas in a pod. It felt good to have a best friend. We had both suffered some hardships in life, but when we were together, we did everything we could to forget about all our problems. We both loved basketball and stayed focused all week, but by the weekend, we were partying all night. The parties of the local kids our age had become monotonous, so we ventured out to other parties with older crowds. My tolerance for alcohol had become quite high, so I would occasionally smoke pot if I needed to numb myself more. Which, by the way, was terrible because I would throw up for hours (I guess I was allergic to it). I could get any guy I wanted to sleep with me. That gave me validation for a moment, but the next day, the hangover was from far more than just the alcohol.

I had to find a way to make money if I wanted to buy makeup and clothes that matched what everyone else was wearing, so I got a job working at the general store. I grew to love working there, and just like everything else in my life, I wanted to be the best at my job. We had lots of tourists come in. I would help them find what they were looking for and tell them about sites to see and things to do around the area. After working there for a while, I even had some regulars that came in and remembered me every time they saw me. It made me feel needed and valued; I craved that feeling more than air. I was like a chameleon. I could blend in wherever I was and play the role I needed to play to fit in. I could be the star on the basketball court, or the life of the party, or the number one employee. But it was becoming harder and harder to keep things under control. My nights of partying had become more frequent and my alcohol use began to tamper with my already unstable moods.

I had become friends with a boy name Sean who lived not too far from me. We were in math class together and I loved being around him. He had a presence about him that I couldn't explain, but it drew me in. After we discovered that we lived close to each other, he offered to pick me up for school and I gladly accepted. We didn't hang out in the same group, but there was something so solid and soothing about him. I knew he went to church, and although he never forced the subject, he seemed to have some sense of peace and joy in his life that I had never experienced.

It sometimes felt like I was just floating from day to day with no anchor. Doing whatever I could to get by, but lost and without any hope of true peace or purpose. I knew there had to be more to life, but I didn't exactly know what it was or how to find it. I would sometimes ask Sean questions about God and Jesus. His answers were so soft and from a place of love. I wanted what he had, but there was no way a God like that could love a girl like me. I enjoyed spending time with Sean, nonetheless. He was so respectful and caring, and never tried to make a move on me. It was as if he just wanted to show me the love of this Jesus guy, expecting nothing in return. As much as I longed for that type of love, I was too full of shame and regret to ask God for forgiveness and help. And it was much cooler to my friends to live the lifestyle of partying rather than going to church. So, I denied the possibility and continued down my path of hopelessness. And still in this place of wanting to be popular and accepted, I was willing to do anything to fit in. I so badly needed validation from people.

By now, I had started driving, which was a new found freedom. My sweet uncle gave me his beat up little Oldsmobile Cutlass Ciera. At school, everyone was getting brand new rides, so this was just another reason I felt like I would never measure up. I thought, "If I just had a new car, I'd be happy." That "If I" phrase is like a silent killer because there will always be something that someone else has that you do not. I wish someone would have told me that before what happened next. This is a moment that destroyed me from the inside out.

One day this "family friend" stopped by the house. He was close to thirty years old and pulled up in a shiny, new, 1996 Blue Ford Ranger. I came running out of the house with an immediate feeling of envy as I looked at the truck. I thought it was so awesome. Then, self-pity began to stir and say, "Poor me, I'll never have a new car or be able to drive a new car." So, we were chatting about his truck and how awesome the sound system was. I sat in the driver's seat, dreaming of what it would be like passing by kids' houses and having them see me out of their window. I just knew they would be so jealous. This thought had me grinning from ear to ear and thinking about how I'd do anything to make this dream a reality. The guy saw me smiling and asked what had me grinning so hard. I responded, "No reason, I was just thinking about how fun it would be to borrow your truck and run some errands." I was practically begging for him to just say, "of course!" With his hands on my lower back, he said, "If you have sex with me, I'll let you drive it for the whole day." My eyes got wide, *"Oh my gosh, what did he just say?"* After that, a million things started running through my mind. Sex is just an act and not emotional, right? Would it hurt? This guy was so much older than anyone I had slept with. I had only slept with boys my age and this guy was double my age. It can't be that much different, right? Plus, this was going to make me the cool kid at school because I was going be behind the wheel of that shiny truck. I continued to try to ration with myself, thinking of all the reasons I could do this. Sex goes fast for guys anyway; I can do anything for a few minutes. So, I mustered up the courage to take my clothes off and laid down.

Y'all, I feel sick as I write these words and relive this pain. It has taken me seven years to write this book because I didn't want the pain of my past to affect who I am now. And there is proof the enemy did not want this part of the book to be written. I had actually already written this part; it was one of the hardest parts to write, and I never thought I would have to write it again. I looked and couldn't find this section anywhere on my computer! Nonetheless, I wrote this again. Not because I still need to release it, but because I want to bring freedom to you.

Back to it. The weight of his body on top of me made my decision real. In an instant, I came to my senses and realized this was a very poor decision. Why would I let this pervert have sex with me just so I could drive his truck for one day in the hopes that it would make me popular? I immediately start yelling, "No, no! I can't do this! I don't want to drive your truck, so please get off of me!" I think you know what comes next. I wouldn't be writing this if he had listened to me. There would be no story to tell here if he didn't force himself onto me, but he did, so here we are. As tears streamed down my face, there was nothing I could do but lay there and hear the words, "This is all your fault because you made this deal." This brief moment of sex seemed like it lasted a lifetime, then it was finally over. I showered right after in an attempt to wash off his smell, and the sadness that was clinging to me. And then, I just got pissed. I became so angry that I let someone hurt me again. But you better believe that I wasn't going to let all of this happen to me and not get the moment I wanted in the first place. By the way, this is not a healthy thought pattern. I went and got his keys off of the counter and left in the new truck. Driving down the road, the moment I was once beaming about, turned into complete horror. I kept replaying the scene of what just happened over and over in my head. How I had told him no and asked him to get off of me. Then I kept hearing again, "This is all your fault." After all, wasn't it really my fault? Hadn't I been the one to say yes in the beginning? Wasn't I the one who took my clothes off? These are the questions that ran through my head every day for years after this moment. Today, I will take responsibility for putting myself and the guy in this position, but he should have gotten up and walked away when I said "no." This is my "me too" moment. This man did not respect my objection and raped me that day. No matter what, this is never, ever, your fault. You cannot blame yourself for the pain someone else caused you. That is why this world is full of so much pain. That is why, as you read this, the flashback of when this happened to you is playing in your mind. This could be like the vivid memories of you being sexually abused by parents, step-parents, siblings, or siblings of a friend. Or it could even be the time you got really drunk at a party and woke up with no clothes on and no memory of what actually happened that night. No matter what your story is, there is healing for you. There is freedom on the other side of the inexcusable pain. And as hard as it may seem, there is forgiveness for the person who caused you the pain.

I would like for you to stop right now and say the following prayer out loud over your life. If you have been abused by anyone in this way, or any way for that matter, regardless of what they said, it is not your fault. I want you to know that it is time to let the shame of it go. Don't let it steal one more day of your life. Don't let it affect how you love or how you receive love. Seek out help from a counselor or trusted pastor to talk about the next step towards healing. You can start by saying this prayer. Know that I am saying it over your life in this moment, too.

God, thank you for creating me in my mother's womb. I know you created me for pureness and wholeness, and you did not cause this abuse. God, I know you want to heal me from the inside out. I know you want to wipe this abuse from my memory and heal me mind, body, and soul. God, only you can touch my body and make it brand new. Only you can create new life apart from abuse. I know you have someone that will love me despite the abuse. I know you love me despite what has happened to me. God, I need you when the pain comes rushing back and I can't breathe. I need you to show me that there is more to me than sexuality and that what happened is not my fault. I know you have the key to release me from these chains. So, in Jesus' name, I release the pain and receive my healing. Thank you for the miracle of restoration. This moment will not define my future. AMEN.

PART II

We are born with a sinful nature. If you doubt that for any reason, think about a two-year-old who does not get their way. You know what I am talking about. When they don't get their way, they fall to the ground and throw a white trash fit. I am currently teaching my one-year-old daughter the word "no." I can say "no" six times, discipline her, and she will still do the thing I was telling her not to do. She is one year old, y'all.

We, as human beings, are no different. We think the grass is always greener on the other side, and if we can just get there we will be happy. Let me just tell you, that is such a lie! Our sinful nature gets a taste of sin and wants more. My first taste of sin was losing my virginity. I felt lost and empty. So if I was going to feel that way, I was going to do enough bad to justify those feelings. Basically, I was trying to find happiness and fill the void in my heart. It did the opposite, though. It made the hole bigger and I lost more of myself, falling deeper into my internal grave, losing site of any light or hope.

This is what God says about emptiness, and the temptations we use to fill the void in our hearts.

1 Corinthians 10:13 NIV - No temptation has overtaken you except what is common to mankind. And God is faithful; he will not let you be tempted beyond what you can bear. But when you are tempted, he will also provide a way out, so you can endure it.

1 John 2:16 NIV - For everything in the world—the lust of the flesh, the lust of the eyes, and the pride of life—comes not from the Father but from the world.

Matthew 26:41 NIV- "Watch and pray so that you will not fall into temptation. The spirit is willing, but the flesh is weak."

Psalm 23 NIV- The Lord is my shepherd, I lack nothing. He makes me lie down in green pastures, he leads me beside quiet waters, He refreshes my soul. He guides me along the right paths for his name's sake. Even though I walk through the darkest valley, I will fear no evil, for you are with me; your rod and your staff, they comfort me. You prepare a table before me in the presence of my enemies. You anoint my head with oil; my cup overflows. Surely your goodness and love will follow me all the days of my life, and I will dwell in the house of the Lord forever.

Psalm 16:11 NIV- You make known to me the path of life; you will fill me with joy in your presence, with eternal pleasures at your right hand.

John 4:10 NIV - "If you only knew the gift God has for you and who you are speaking to, you would ask me, and I would give you living water."

Here Jesus is talking about giving us "the living water." He goes on to say that if we drink of the living water, we will never thirst again! Wow! I was so thirsty to be wanted. I was looking for something to satisfy my soul in all of those men. I would feel wanted for the night, but would wake feeling more empty than the last time. How many of us are searching to satisfy our appetite? It's so sad that wedding vows don't really even matter anymore. It is as simple as looking around at your job. You can sneak around with a co-worker and temporarily satisfy your needs, and if no one finds out, you think no one will get hurt. I am here to testify that people do get hurt. The truth will always come out. Light will flush out the darkness and that means the truth will flush out the lie. There are so many things that can happen to make this come about. Jealousy, fear, curiosity, or even the simple fact that we can't live with the lies anymore. It will come out. The enemy uses our mind to convince us that what we are doing is okay. The enemy lies to us and points us in the wrong direction. It is not until we have searched for happiness in all of the wrong places that we actually look up and start searching God's word to find out about His living water. We don't need anything else. His grace is so beautiful. There is an unlimited supply, and it is powerful enough to cover every single past regret. Every single one.

Seven

BROKENNESS
PART I

bro·ken·ness

The state or quality of being broken: Separated into parts or pieces by violence;
divided into fragments; Fractured; cracked; disunited; sundered; strained; Crushed
and ruined as by something that destroys hope; blighted.[5]

Senior year was different than the years before. I started the year on top of my game. I had figured out what my strengths were and how to use them to get what I wanted. Basketball and boys were my primary focus, and I was good at both. I was getting a lot of recognition for basketball and had even been featured in the local paper for throwing five three-pointers in one game. I was kind of a big deal, and I was savoring every moment of attention.

When I wasn't on the court perfecting my skills, I was partying and hopping around from guy to guy. I had pretty much gone through all the guys in my grade, so I had to look elsewhere for my next target. We had just voted for yearbook awards and I won multiple categories. I was proud to hold the title of "biggest flirt" and even more proud to get voted "best eyes." There happened to be an eleventh-grade guy who won "best eyes" as well. I had noticed him before, and his mysterious nature had me intrigued. His name was Brian and he was different than most of the guys I dated. He had long hair, the style of a heavy metal musician, and kept to himself. I never knew him to date anyone, so he became my new challenge. In the beginning, he didn't show interest. So I started partying with him and his brother. They lived on their own, so that was fun. I always got the men I wanted, so Brian was no different. But this relationship would end differently.

At this point I had quit working at the general store and went to work with Brian at the Fish Nest before we started dating. But once we started dating, I remember his momma telling us, "She better get on birth control or y'all are going to get pregnant." I remember this like it was yesterday. I knew quickly that I didn't want that, so I went to the health clinic and got on birth control. What she said scared me, because after all, I had been having sex for three years and not thought twice about the pill or protection.

At the health clinic they gave me a brown bag full of condoms and I was like, "We can use these to make sure I don't get pregnant before the pill kicks in." We had only been dating for two months, but it was normal for me to sleep with someone on the first date. And that first night, we used the condom, but it broke. I went into the bathroom and cried because I knew in that moment that I was going to be pregnant. I prayed and asked God to fix it. That was the only time I would ever pray or talk to God. It was always when I was in a desperate situation or wanted something from Him. Brian and I kept partying like nothing had happened. Honestly, I completely put that night out of my mind. Everything was confirmed when I was in the club around Christmas and I smelled a perfume so strongly it made me sick. The next day I took a pregnancy test. The word on it was "positive." I took three more and they all said the same thing. Positive. I was positively pregnant and I was positively scared out of my mind. Brian mentioned having an abortion, but that wasn't an option for me. Again, deep inside, I knew better. You might ask, "Were you really surprised that it was positive?" And the answer would be a resounding, "no." I had been doing what everyone else was doing, I just finally got caught and there was no hiding it.

By now, I had been attending the local community college for a semester. Honestly, I liked college and I did pretty well, but my life was changing in this moment. So, Brian and I worked together at the Fish Nest while I was pregnant. What should be the next move? A ring? Maybe move in together? We did what we thought was best (which is usually never best), and we moved in together. We played house and worked a lot.

Again, thinking we knew what was best, we actually picked up everything we had and moved six hours away to Runaway Bay, Texas. No, that is not a joke. We ran away to Runaway Bay. How fitting. It was actually beautiful! We had a trailer on the lake and he had a good job. Brian had family there in town, his dad and three cousins. They were so nice to us. It all seemed like it was going to turn out well, but the key word there is seemed. I was playing house, trying to make a happy family. The problem is that I was being something that I was not. I was a very good actress, and I was dominating this role. The days passed and before I knew it, I was giving birth to a beautiful 7lb, 1oz baby boy. We named him Ozzie. It was the perfect day. My best friend, Jennifer, drove to see me, and surprisingly, my mom came with her. She still hadn't been a big part of my life, so I thought it was awesome that she came. My dad came too. That moment was all about me and Ozzie.

The first night home was a feeling I will never forget. I had no idea what just happened to my body, and even more, I had no idea how I was going to take care of this tiny human. I went on, but the days were long and the nights were longer. Brian would go off to work and I was stuck in the trailer all day thinking about how my life used to be. The parties, the clubs, the friends, the attention. Quite frankly, I hated it. It was just me, and I had to give all of my time and attention to this baby, and I wasn't getting anything. Selfishness at its finest. So, what did I do after six weeks of this? I cracked. I told Brian that I needed to go to Arkansas to see my dad. I really just wanted to go party, and that is exactly what I did. To top it off, I had just been released by the doctor to have sex again. Brian had not been made aware of this because I wasn't happy with him anymore, and I had no intention of doing that with him. I ended up sleeping with this random guy I met, or at least trying to sleep with him. Those of us who have had a baby know that the first time after is not the best of times. So now I had this secret. I had torn my family apart, Brian just didn't know it. The secret was mine, but, as they always do, it was killing me. I had a taste of my old life and the old freedom. I wanted more of it.

To no one's surprise, once I got back to Runaway Bay, things began to quickly decline between me and Brian. I wanted to move back home, and he was actually willing to do it because he thought it would make me happy. He didn't know it, but it was actually going to be the ending to our "happily ever after." I thought since we weren't married, that justified everything and meant I wasn't a terrible person. We went back to working at the Fish Nest, but this time it was different. We hated each other, but had this cute little baby. Brian got angry and more violent with me. I would be out all night while he had Ozzie. He was at his breaking point. I'll never forget the night he grabbed me by the neck, leaned me over our kitchen table, and you know what happened next. I am not saying that I didn't provoke him to do that. I did. I wanted him to hurt me, so that I wouldn't be the "bad mom," or the one who was at fault for splitting up the family.

Over the next few months, my partying and drinking got worse, the shame I carried from sleeping around was too much to bear, and I was exhausted from trying to keep the family together. I decided that I needed to move out. I moved in with Jennifer, and I partied when I didn't have Ozzie.

During this season of partying, I ended up meeting and ultimately dating a guy who was wrapped up in drugs. He was so dark, perverse, and enticing. He had control over me in a way that I can't even explain. He actually hadn't done drugs in front of me, but I knew he was "off." Sexually, we did the worst of things. He could talk me into things and lead me to a place there just aren't words for. We even recorded movies of us having sex. He was Fifty Shades Darker before that was a novel. You see, I had been "bad" before. I had done plenty of bad things, but after having a baby, not being the mom I knew I needed to be, and having Brian's anger thrown at me all of the time, I just felt so alone. This guy wanted me, so I willingly walked into his darkness, over and over again. Of course, I repeated the pattern and slept with someone else, screwing up that relationship. Afterwards, I wanted this guy back so badly. His darkness was like a magnet. I couldn't resist it and I wanted that lifestyle back. I wanted the dysfunction and perverseness back. But, he said no. He was cold to me. I was shocked. No one had ever been able to resist my games. No one had ever turned me down.

It was the end of April and I knew that he was going to Memphis in May. I talked his friend into taking me with them, knowing there was no way I wouldn't get him back if I went. What I couldn't foresee was how this trip would change my life forever.

PART II

The circumstances that you try to create with your own power will never fix you, like a baby will never complete you. I honestly thought that it would. I thought that if I could be something that my mom wasn't, my life would be complete and I'd be happy. When that didn't happen, I was left broken. How could I put my life back together when I had become the one person I didn't want to be? I wish I had known about God's grace, and that His grace was all I needed to accept to be able to move forward with my life. Really, what if I would have grasped what God's grace is? What if I had understood what salvation was all about? Would I have been seeking my worth and value in men? Would have I have felt like I was too far gone for God to want me? You see, grace is something you don't deserve or earn, it is what He freely gives to us. So, the picture in my head is of me, laying there in a million broken pieces, and I watch His grace put the pieces back together. It makes something so beautiful out of the things that I had broken or the world had broken. Of course, that is the whole point to me writing this book. I don't want you to go as far down into the pit as I did. It's like when you say, "Life can't get any worse," and then it somehow does. That was me, but it doesn't have to be your story. Reading this may save you from destroying your life further. You can accept what God has done for you at this moment. His grace will lead you to have great faith that there is someone to pick up your pieces. He can and He will. The proof is in the Bible.

2 Corinthians 12:8-9 NIV- Three times I pleaded with the Lord to take it away from me. But He said to me, "My grace is sufficient for you, my power is made perfect in weakness." Therefore I will boast all the more gladly, so that Christ's power may rest on me.

Romans 3:23-24 NIV- For all have sinned and fall short of the glory of God, and all are justified freely by His grace through the redemption that came by Jesus Christ.

Ephesians 2:8-9 NIV- For by grace you have been saved through faith- and this is not from yourselves, it is the gift of God; not by works, so that no one can boast.

Romans 6:14 NIV- For sin shall no longer be your master because you are not under the law, but under grace.

John 1:16 NIV- Out of His fullness we have all received grace in place of grace already given.

As you will come to see, I didn't accept His grace when I needed it most.

HOPELESS

PART I

hope·less·ness

Having no expectation of goodness or success.[5]

By now you know that one dysfunctional thought leads to another. Just like addiction leads to emptiness, and emptiness to brokenness, brokenness leads to feeling hopeless. When you can't satisfy your hunger you will try anything. At this point you become hopeless in feeling that your life will be anything other than miserable. This is when you begin to think, "What does it matter anyway? I've already thrown my life away, so why change?" or, "I have no purpose or hope for my future." People die all the time in this state because they can't see past their hopelessness. That was almost my story, but it wasn't, and that is why I want to tell it to you.

It was the weekend of May 4th and I was in Memphis. We had gone to Memphis because it was Memphis in May, a popular music festival. There were bands everywhere. We saw The Dave Matthews Band, Lynyrd Skynyrd, and more drunk people than sober ones. The "hoochier" your clothes were, the more you fit in with the crowd. It was the life for a partier like me. I mean, there were famous bands, alcohol, and lots of men who were willing to give me the attention I wanted. But, for some reason I wanted to win this one guy back. This guy who had a huge hold over my emotions and life. Remember, he didn't want anything to do with me because I had slept with someone else and ruined the way he felt about me, like I had done with so many other relationships. My thought process was, "If he sees me having a really rad time with his friends, it may strike interest up again." So, I was going to do whatever it took. We had a

 [6]Merriam-webster.com

full day of drinking and partying on this particular day, before going back into the hotel room. This was not a nice hotel. We were just sitting in this dark room with only the lamps shining on the tables. That's when it happened. They pulled out this white stuff and started chopping it up and making into thin lines. Their exact words to me were, "Hey, we are about to do this." It was as nonchalant as it could have been, as if, "this" was not a big deal.

I asked what "this" was, and they answered, "Meth, but you don't want any." In desperation, I told them I did! I thought this boy wouldn't give me any attention otherwise, so I would show him by getting high, and he would realize how fun and loose I could be. They handed me the tube and told me to snort. It was like my first sip of alcohol, that first time watching my dad's VHS tape, and definitely like losing my virginity. It is actually surprising, sadly, that there was still something I could try for the first time by the time I was nineteen. Leading up to this, I was fearless and didn't care if I lived or died, so trying meth was no different. Of course I thought, "Maybe this will make it all go away, all of my pain and unhappiness, because life can't get any worse, right?" So, I said, "Here we go... Let's do this!" It burned as it slid down the back of my throat, and then, euphoria. A rush like never before. The hairs on my head stood up. I could feel my eyes dilating and bulging out. The tingles went from the top of my head to the bottoms of my feet. My mind was as clear as it had ever been. I felt on top of the world, y'all, and I felt like I could save the world. Now, the music sounded better, the alcohol tasted better, and I felt sexier. What I didn't realize is I sold myself to the devil right then. The demons I had before were nothing compared to the demons I would fight with this addiction. I thought I had issues before, but this magnified them. It magnified all of the hurt I had experienced. It is all fun and games when you're high, but just like the saying goes, everything that goes up must come down, and coming down from meth ain't no joke. It is like hitting concrete after jumping out of a thirty story building. Of course, that didn't stop me from loving it and wanting it at all costs. I didn't want to do anything but get high. I didn't care about anyone or anything other than that white powder. You could find me at the club every night, high, feeling very sexy and sleeping around with whomever. I knew that even though I didn't always have the money to buy it, I could "sell" one more piece of my body for it.

One night I was at the club and met a new guy. He was a singer in the band that night and to no surprise, I wanted his attention. So we partied with them for a bit and he eventually asked me out. He said, "I got some good stuff if you want to go get high." That is how easy it was to ask me out; you could clearly see "druggie" written all over my face. This decision was the final nail in my coffin. Over the course of the next four months, I would literally spiral out of control. My answer to him was, "Yes, let's go!" I had just met this guy, but he had the new love of my life, meth. He had the thing that was making me temporarily happy, and I had what he wanted. For a while, this took all of my problems away. Come to find out, he was a drug dealer. So, I quickly became his side-kick, doing whatever he needed me to do, just so I could maintain my own high. For breakfast, I would have a couple of lines. For lunch, a couple of lines. And supper, a couple of lines. You get the picture. I was feeding myself meth. In the beginning, it was fun. I could have as much as I wanted, and all I had to do was satisfy him sexually. But, somehow, deep down, I knew this couldn't be my lot. This couldn't be my story. I left my child, abandoned him just like my mom did, and even her mom had. Ozzie would pop into my head and I would feel like a failure. There was so much guilt and shame when I would come down from the high. I thought I had suicidal thoughts before being addicted to meth, but those were nothing compared to the thoughts I had coming down off of this demon drug. Thankfully, I never put my thoughts into action.

Time passed and something in this guy shifted one day. A few things that always come with this lifestyle are abuse, fear, and cops. So, before I had lost everything and before my son's father knew how bad I was, I decided that I couldn't live this life anymore. I knew I had to get away. Obviously, when you are talking about a drug dealer, it isn't as easy as saying, "I need to get away." To be even more transparent, I didn't even think my addiction was the problem, I just knew my problem was the fact that I was connected to a freaking drug dealer. Lord knows how, but I still had my car at this time, so in my irrational thinking while high, I planned to run away from it all and go get clean with my brother in Colorado. That is how I planned to put my life back together. And I had planned to do this all within a matter of days, because who likes to wait or stay in the midst of pain when we are trying to change? Despite all of this, I still had a love for meth more than I had love for anything else. I had tricked myself into thinking that it hadn't taken everything from me yet, so I wasn't that bad off. Great thinking, Jessica. Really though, why would I think any other way? I wasn't raised to speak life or truth over myself. No one had done that to me. I didn't know that was a way of life. I just let the world carry me away to its darkest happily ever after, minus the "happily" part.

I made it to Denver, but by the time I got there I needed to get high again. As selfish as I was, thinking it was all about me, I asked my brother to find meth for me. What is worse, my brother wasn't a drug addict, but he was a drunk. I was so happy when he got some for me and to make matters worse, I convinced him to do a line with me, "Come on, Bobby, it will be a bonding experience." Those were my words, and that was my thought pattern. Of course, Bobby said yes. He didn't tell me, "No, sis, I have a great life in Denver. I have a great job and a great girlfriend. I am actually the best I have ever been." He didn't say those things, even though they were true; his life was great in Denver. He ended up getting high with me for the first time. Y'all, meth isn't kind. It doesn't say, "Okay Bobby, since you are just bonding with your sister, I won't grip you like a python. I won't play in your ears over and over until you come find more of me. I won't shake your body until you get your fix. I will spare you from all of the havoc I cause." No, meth is no respecter of persons. As you will come to find out, or may already know, it kills, steals, and destroys. It's literally the devil, with no pitch fork or red horns; it is just a simple, white powder.

I convinced myself that I wasn't as bad off anymore, because at least I was doing drugs with my brother and not the drug dealer. The first thing to do with my new life was to get a job so I could keep buying. You know when you are asked as a little kid, "What do you want to be when you grow up?" My answer was always, "A coach, hairstylist, or secretary." I never said, "A stripper." I had danced a few times at a club in Hot Springs, and quickly realized it was a feeling I never wanted to have again. So, what in the world was I thinking?! I concluded that it was a feeling I never wanted to have again while I was sober. Surely, it wouldn't feel the same if I was dancing while being high. With meth coursing through my veins, I could definitely make my body work for it, and it would make the money I needed.

So, we headed to a couple of the biggest strip clubs. None of them would hire me because I wasn't twenty-one yet, but then the last place said I could come dance for them. This place wasn't the classiest of all of them, but I didn't care. I left there, and went and got high. I thought to myself, *"You are making it now Jessica. You are moving up in the world."* I was supposed to start there soon, but then my little pre-paid phone rang and I answered. It was the drug dealer, and he was missing me. He was begging me to come home and be with him. I said, "I have changed! But, if you show up to Denver and buy meth for me, I will go home with you." I remember so vividly the words, "I am on my way." I didn't think he would really make it there. Really, I didn't think he wanted me that badly. Heck, everyone else had left me, so why would he go so far out of his way to get me?

It was about control. When he showed up, he knew that I would leave my car with my brother, and then I would have no way of leaving him again. He knew he was walking me into his prison cell and he had the key to my life. So, we drove around Denver before heading back. Being with him this time was different. He had a different kind of meth and it was making me really happy, really quickly. Crystal meth. It was the new love of my life. We called it "ice." Y'all, it was so powerful. But, someone forgot to mention it is a stimulant that causes rage and makes you psycho. It doesn't come with a warning label. There is nothing that says, "When you and your drug dealer boyfriend take this for days upon days, you will try to kill each other." Basically, this drug was making an abusive man even more abusive.

We drove from Denver to Arkansas and we ended up at a house around Little Rock. He didn't have a job, so dealing became his life. I couldn't tell you how we ended up at this particular house. I was so wasted by the time we got there, and I stayed in that state for the next three months. The only thing I knew was the trailer that we were staying at belonged to a cocaine dealer and he was never home. If he ever came home, I didn't know it, because I was confined to the bedroom. I would only come out now and then to eat a few animal crackers. I was like an animal locked in its cage. My boyfriend would come home, get me high, get what he needed from me, and go back out to the streets. On average, I would sleep probably 24 hours in a week and eat actual food every three days. It was special for him to bring home McDonalds for me to eat. But more than anything, he always had meth for me, and for that, I was satisfied. Until I came down from the high again. When I was down, I dreamed of running out in front of a car that was going 100 miles per hour, hoping it would ease my pain.

If you are the drug dealer, you don't do the drugs that you are supposed to be selling. I thought this was common sense, but my boyfriend didn't put that one together. Doing so will likely come to a point where the drug lord shows up, putting a gun to your head. This actually happened a few times and it had become so dangerous that we had to hide out and not resurface for a few days. During these hideout moments, we couldn't get high as often as we needed to, so it became very toxic. Our fights were louder and his hands became more violent. Somehow, he would figure it out and find something to get us through. We usually had to mix what he could find with caffeine powder to get the high we so badly desired. One day, he went out to get more because I was withdrawing pretty badly. I was panicking and starting to think about things that I didn't want to think about. To numb the pain, I just started inhaling the caffeine powder, eating it in spoonfuls like cereal. I even went as far as to put it in a light bulb, like a make-shift pipe, and smoke it out of there. At first, nothing seemed to be happening, but then it did. My heart started racing and my body sweating. It felt like a car was on my chest and I couldn't breathe. In that moment, I thought that was the end. And I didn't even care. I was overdosing and my body was shutting down. But, for the first time in a while, I thought of my son. I thought of his sky blue eyes and sandy blonde hair. I could see his smile and hear his laugh. I started screaming on the inside, "Wait, wait! I don't want to die like this! I don't want to be remembered as a meth addict with sores all over my body and my face sunken in!" You see, my son was about to turn one, and even though he didn't know it, his own mother was getting ready to die, not getting ready for his party.

How did I get here? How did a little party lead to me lying in this bed dying? I was trashed and I had lost everything. Well, I didn't die that day, but of course, at the time I didn't care. I made my way to the kitchen to eat something and try to soak up some of the powder that I had taken in. My boyfriend got home and I told him what happened. He started yelling at me like it was my fault, and he made sure that I knew I was going to pay. Not because he cared about me, but because if I died he would have to pay for that. He was angry, screaming at me, forcing me to have sex with him, and we didn't go to sleep that night. He got me high again so that I would forget about his hatred and what he had just done to me.

I came to my senses the next day and realized I had to get home. It was time for me to see my son. I hadn't physically seen him in months. He only existed in my thoughts at that point. So, I told my boyfriend that I needed to go home and get well. I'm sure you can guess, but that is the wrong thing to say to a controlling drug addict. He started telling me about what he had done to his ex-girlfriend and said the same thing would happen to me if I left him. What he didn't think about was that I didn't care if I got hurt or not. I was living in hell anyway, so the best thing he could do for me was to kill me and put me out of my misery. There was no way he was going to hurt me any more than how I was feeling inside. So, I ran out the door as fast as someone in my condition could. Y'all, it was literally like a scene from a movie, but it was my life, and it was real. I made it outside and the air was so thick and still. I looked around and it was like the trees were talking to me. The demons were screaming at me so loudly my ears were ringing. It was so loud I couldn't hear what my boyfriend was saying as he followed me outside.

My brain was so foggy from everything I had put in my body, and from all of the drama and fear that was surrounding me. I turned around and he was standing right in front of me. His face was like nothing I had never seen before. It was literally like the devil had taken over his face. The look in his eyes was unreal. It was worse than a horror movie. I felt it all, but in slow motion. His hands started to raise and he wrapped them around my neck. He lifted me off the ground and threw me down like a rag doll. There I was, beaten and bruised. I couldn't move. Tears were streaming down my face, and I remember feeling how warm they were. That reminded me that I was still alive. I knew that if I didn't leave him that day, I was going to end up dead. He had nothing to lose, and I was an easy target for his violent, meth-induced outbursts.

The thing with drugs, specifically meth for me, is that they make you like a dog that returns to its own vomit. You think about getting help when times are terrible, but then it is so crazy how quickly you forget the pain. I know that I made it away from my drug dealer boyfriend, but I just made my way to my other drug-ridden friends and started partying with them. I couldn't get out of bed most days because they weren't giving me enough meth to give me the energy or motivation to move. I remember a day when someone came in my room to wake me up. I had no idea how many days I had even been asleep. Thinking back to all of this, I can still feel the numbness and the sores in my mouth. The sores were so bad, I could barely talk. Anyway, someone came in, shook me, and said, "Jess, Jess, wake up, we have something for you, but you have to get out of this bed." I was like, "If it ain't meth, I ain't moving." So, I opened my eyes long enough to see this blurred vision of "the love of my life." They had gotten me the good stuff and there were two lines just for me.

I still had glimpses of wanting to change, but also felt like I was too far gone to change. I mean, how can I change a life that I had destroyed? How is change possible when you can't even get out of bed without getting high? I believed the lie that once you're in that world you can never get out. So, you won't believe what I did... Well, you actually probably will. In my hopeless state, I went back to my boyfriend, the drug dealer. This is the part of the movie that everyone hates. This is the part where we all stop pitying the person, and basically think, "Well, if they are stupid enough to do that, then they deserve what's coming." Hear me out, though. He told me that he had really changed (insert eye-rolling emoji here). He gave me that crappy lie, and I chose to believe it.

No matter how bad off I was as a meth addict, I always denied that I had a problem. I denied it all, convincing myself that I didn't have a problem and that I had control of my life. I can't even describe how strong of a hold this dysfunction had on me. So, I moved back in with him, into a studio apartment in Hot Springs. I remember that we had a few dishes and a mattress, but that was it. He told me that he was no longer doings drugs, and I convinced myself that I was sober. He was so manipulative; he "dropped" a bag of crystal and didn't realize it. C'mon, we all know he knew that I would smoke it. And as predicted, that little baggy was all mine the second he left me alone. He eventually came home and I went psycho on him for lying to me and he went psycho on me for using his drugs. Everything we had in us rose up in this fight. All of the violence and anger we had for each other. All of the drama from before came raging back in his mind, and he pulled a knife on me. Yep, I knew it. That was it. He was about to kill me for real, no doubt about it. But... the fighter in me came out. I got so pissed. I had gotten away once just to get back into this hell all over again. I remembered that I was the mother to a little boy, and something inside me decided to rise up and fight! I knew that I had a bigger purpose than the life I had been living. Here we go with another movie scene... I made a fist with my right hand, and in what again felt like slow motion, I brought my fist around and punched him in the face. I immediately ran into the bathroom and he came banging on the door, threatening my life, for what felt like three hours. I don't know why, but eventually, he left. In that bathroom, I cried out to God. As my boyfriend was beating on the door, I said, "God, if you are real, then you will get me out of this situation, but not just out of dying this day, but every day of my life. You will save me from the death that is on the inside of me. God, can I be more than a meth addicted whore? Can I be more than someone who has psychotic episodes every day of her life?"

PART II

When you are in the midst of an addiction, the enemy wants you to feel too far gone, to feel like you're in the bottom of the pit. I know you may feel you are at the end of your rope, but trust me, that is actually a better place to be rather than convincing yourself everything is fine. When I was using, I couldn't admit that I was an addict. When I was sleeping around with everyone, I couldn't admit that I was a slut. But when I truly came to my knees and admitted I was hopeless, that is when God could even begin to show up in my life. The truth is what sets us free. We can be freed from the prison, even if we are the ones that put ourselves there.

John 8:32 NIV- "Then you will know the truth, and the truth will set you free."

Revelation 21:4 NIV- He will wipe away every tear from their eyes. There will be no more death, or mourning or crying or pain, for the old order of things has passed away.

Matthew 11:28-30 NIV - "Come to me, all you who are weary and burdened, and I will give you rest. Take my yoke upon you and learn from me, for I am gentle and humble in heart, and you will find rest for your souls. For my yoke is easy and my burden is light."

Romans 15:13 NIV- May the God of hope fill you with all joy and peace as you trust in him, so that you may overflow with hope by the power of the Holy Spirit.

Psalm 71:14 NIV- As for me, I will always have hope; I will praise you more and more.

Nine

GETTING SOBER SUCKS
PART I

Your hopelessness will either bring you death or it will give you the strength to change. I wanted rest, but not just sleep. I wanted all the weight of my baggage to disappear, to be taken off my back. I needed to go on a soul search and figure out who I was born to be before these drugs told me who I was. Freedom wasn't happening overnight, but I knew there had to be more to life than the way I was living. Up to this point, though, I was just surviving minute to minute. Is there even a God and does He even care? Would my life ever change? Could I be more than this girl sitting on the floor in the corner shaking? Could I be any different than the forty- and fifty-year-old women who are still sleeping around to get their next fix?

There had always been a sort of angel in my life running around Kirby, Arkansas. Her name was Janna Ray. She would pop in and out of my life. When I was younger and thinking that I could be a model, she cared enough to take me out and take photos of me, just helping me live out that dream. I can't image what she thought when rumors were swarming around Kirby about how bad I had gotten, or that I had not even seen my son in the last couple of months. I can't imagine the prayers she was praying, hoping that I would make it out alive. Thankfully, Janna was not the type to judge. She was living for God and did exactly what He told her to do. I think my dad knew that about her. She was such a blessing to my life. When I was on my way to detox, my dad didn't know what to do, so he stopped by Janna's work to let her know he rescued me and it didn't look good. I asked Janna to put in her words a bit of what she saw that day. It is unreal, y'all. Reading her words has tears falling down my face. No one is born and dreams of their life turning out like this. We don't want to fall on our faces, but life knocks us down and sometimes it gets really bad before it gets better. This is Janna's part of the story.

A familiar face opened the door at the little store where I worked. "Hi, Jerry." His dark brown eyes twinkled at me above the ZZ Top beard. He quietly, in true Jerry-style, picked out his purchases and I rang him up. After the transaction, he paused. "I've got Jessica in the car."

Jessica. The beautiful teenager with whom I had struck up an unlikely friendship. The girl whose sparkling personality and gorgeous looks prophesied an amazing future. The girl who had been willfully missing for weeks, maybe months. My heart pounded as I followed Jerry out the door and to the car. As I opened the car door my breath caught in my throat as I tried to hide my disbelief. The person crumpled in the seat was all but unrecognizable. Her once gorgeous ebony hair hung in long, matted clumps. Her fingers with dirty black nails wiped at tears that streamed down her face. Her entire body was trembling. If she'd had anything to eat lately, it wasn't much. "Hey, girl." Her response was hoarse and her eyes stayed down. I told her I loved her and she nodded. No words were needed. "I'm glad you're home." She nodded again. I shut the door and watched Jerry head out, taking his baby girl home. My heart was both full and heavy for the rest of the day. Full for the prodigal that had come home. I didn't know details, but they didn't matter. Heavy because I had avoided the opportunity to witness to Jessica about the Lord in past years - my own life riddled with mistakes and insecurities that Satan freely used against me. Lord, I don't know what to say or do. You know I get tonguetied. I don't have the spiritual gifts to be a witness. My own life is not in order. Why would anyone listen to me? Still, I felt a tugging to go to her. (Isn't the Holy Spirit just something else?) Stuff. I will bring her stuff. I will go and I will bring her a Dr. Pepper and a barbecue sandwich. That girl did love her some Dr. Pepper and barbecue sandwiches. My great idea turned to disappointment as I saw how small and insignificant the bag looked. There needed to be more stuff. Girly stuff. I picked out some lotion and a journal and headed over to see my friend. As we visited, the words wouldn't come. Lord, this isn't the right time. She just needs a friend. Can't I just be a friend? She knows I'm a Christian. Maybe she'll want to become one, too. And the words never came. But I told her I loved her no matter what. There was no judgment from me.

Can we just pause for a minute after reading what Janna said about the condition I was in? Imagine how my dad was feeling. For months he didn't talk to me because he said that if I was going to be a drug addict, he wasn't going to support me. Yes, he kept loving me. Was that the best thing for him to do? Absolutely, yes! I needed to lose everything, and having my dad not talk to me showed me how bad I really was. It showed me that I truly disappointed the man who gave his life to raise me when my mom bolted. The man who worked any job he could to provide for me and my brother. It was never my daddy's fault that I turned out the way I had. He didn't know how to raise a girl. Crap, how many of us really know how to raise children, period? Janna briefly mentioned it in her story, but my dad was just like the father of the prodigal son in the Bible. You should definitely read that after you finish this. You will find it ironically similar. My dad was right there waiting for me to call and admit that I needed him. He was waiting for me to say, "Daddy take me home, I want to rest." He never stopped loving me. He did the hardest thing he ever had to do, and that was to give tough love. He set aside his own feelings to push me to my breaking point.

So we got to Dad's on September 6th and I went to sleep. This wasn't your average eight hour sleep cycle. No, this was like that dead-sleep. I didn't wake up for about a day and a half. When I did finally wake up, I couldn't even lift my head because I was so sick and weak. Life had to continue moving forward for my dad, so he had gone to work. It was just me, all alone. Why couldn't I have a mom to take care of me when I was sick? Why couldn't my life be normal? Even as I write this, I still think, "Where the heck were you, mom? Your daughter was lying on that bed, practically dead! Why couldn't you be there to wash my face, brush my hair, or hold my hand? Surely, in twenty-one years, you could have found your own healing enough to walk me through this." But that wasn't the case. So, all my thoughts of self-pity came rushing back lying in that bed.

I had to pee. How was I going to get to the bathroom if I couldn't even lift my head? I got up the courage to roll out of the bed and onto the floor. Crying and thinking, "Wow, how did I get to this point?" A girl who was once healthy, athletic, and playing basketball, to a weak girl who can't even walk to the bathroom. I managed to get on my hands and knees and crawled to the bathroom. Once I made it back to my bed, I went back to sleep. When I woke up on the third day, I wanted to get high. Screw detoxing, it is too hard, and it would be easier to snort or smoke something that would give me the strength to go on. As these thoughts consumed me, I heard a faint knock on my door. My voice sounded like Rose, from Titanic, as she yelled for the boats to come back for her. I worked up the power to speak and said, "Come in!" It was my earthly angel Janna Ray, with a book and lotion in her hands. This lotion was the best thing I had ever smelled. Maybe because I hadn't showered in weeks, or because it was the smell of hope for me. To this day, I can get a whiff of that smell and it brings me back to God's faithfulness in the midst of my doubt and unbelief. The book spoke to the one thing that I had been thinking; it spoke to my thoughts of quitting. I was ready to give up on the whole "getting sober" thing. I looked down at the front of the book, and these two small words jumped out at me: Don't Quit.

I felt like for the first time, God said, "Jessica, I see you and it's going to be okay. I am right here and I am going to carry you through this pain. You don't have to focus on not having a mom. I will send you exactly what you need, the moment you need it." In that moment, a little bit of the hopelessness I had been carrying disappeared. The veil was pulled back from my eyes enough that I could see Jesus was the one standing at the door and knocking. But believe me, things weren't suddenly peachy. Actually, it was quite the opposite. It was one of the hardest battles I had faced to date. It was the battle of doing what I didn't want to do, and not doing what I promised God I would do if he rescued me out of that pit. So after Janna left that day, I continued to rest. I took a shower and grabbed some food. I started sitting up in my bed, and read the front of that book every day. The first day I had started feeling a little bit more like my old self, that drug dealer boyfriend showed up to my house. It was Sept 11, 2001. Oddly, I wasn't afraid of him. It was a weird phase I was going through. I let him take me on his motorcycle to get food. When we got to the store, I looked up at the TV and saw airplanes running into the buildings in New York. I looked around the room and there was no air in it. People were just looking around zombie-like. I wondered if in this moment I was hallucinating from the detox, or maybe this guy slipped me some drugs. But neither one was true; this was really happing. My first day of freedom equaled turmoil for the rest of the world. I was sober and I think for the first time he may have been healthy, too. But I knew I wasn't going to move forward in my journey with him, so he took me back to the top of the hill to my dad's house. We gave each other this weird, peaceful hug and he left. I think I may have seen him one other time, but other than that, he was a distant memory (or should I say distant nightmare). I wouldn't trade the nightmare for anything, because for the first time I was searching for how to really live and be whole. I was searching for Heaven. It had to be real because after all, I had experienced Hell.

PART II

You see, though, that was just the beginning of hope. The next year was actually another year from hell. I didn't find the freedom I had hoped to find after that first detox. As I have said, it is like a dog that returns to their own vomit; I relapsed over and over again. Something that I love about the Bible is that it is not only life-giving, but there are also scriptures that speak directly to how you are feeling. It reminds you that you are not alone where you are. The scriptures I am sharing so perfectly describe the turmoil I was living in and the battle I was facing.

Romans 7:15-17 NLT- I don't really understand myself, for I want to do what is right, but I don't do it. Instead, I do what I hate. But if I know that what I am doing is wrong, this shows that I agree that the law is good. So I am not the one doing wrong; it is sin living in me that does it.

This first translation is in the New Living Translation, but I am also going to share The Message Translation because it is a little more in-your-face, which is what we need sometimes.

Romans 7:14-16 MSG – I can anticipate the response that is coming: "I know that all God's commands are spiritual, but I'm not. Isn't this also your experience?" Yes. I'm full of myself—after all, I've spent a long time in sin's prison. What I don't understand about myself is that I decide one way, but then I act another, doing things I absolutely despise. So if I can't be trusted to figure out what is best for myself and then do it, it becomes obvious that God's command is necessary.

Initially, I was living with my dad during the detox. Two months had passed and I had gotten a job at Claire's, but then I was fired for smoking in the break room. Friends would let me sleep on their couches over the next two months, as I was partying again and not focusing on moving forward with my sobriety. I knew I needed to take the next step to give me something to live for, a purpose to get up for every day and stay sober. So, one day I was outside and I looked over and saw this poster board. *Oh my gosh, it's my science project from 4th grade about wanting to be a cosmetologist!* I knew immediately that this was a sign from The Lord that cosmetology had to be my next step. But, when you are about to step into something healthy that moves you into your purpose, the enemy has a way of bringing distractions into your life. One of my good friends had messed around in the drug world, and I would beg him to get me high (remember, relapse after relapse). The crazy thing was, this friend of mine would get high, but he wouldn't let me get high. At the time it would make me so mad! He did cave a few times, but when it was over, he always made a point to remind me that this life wasn't for me.

I want to say thank you to that friend, "Ackdog," for believing in me when I didn't believe in myself. We never dated; we were just good friends. I bet you are wondering if I ever slept with him, and surprisingly, that answer is no. It was a miracle that a guy respected me that much and that sex with me wasn't his only goal. He just genuinely cared about me. He would take me to his mom's house because she cared about me, too. Bonnie, his mom, was the first mother figure to take me in and mother me. We would sit on her porch for hours and she would talk to me about my future and life. She would look at me like I was going to change the world, and she thought I hung the moon. Which didn't make sense then, but now I know it was what you call "unconditional love." One day she confirmed what I had seen that day outside. She looked at me and said, "Jessica, you need to do hair." I heard that loud and clear, and acted it on right then.

I drove to the local beauty school. I was both nervous and scared, because I still was very socially awkward and still had the effects of being a drug addict lingering on my face and body. Would she notice? Would she ask? Would drugs be the reason my life never goes forward? This fear was so real, but I am just crazy enough to push past those fears. I made it to the school, walked in, and there was the sweetest girl at the front desk. Her name was Julie and she had a soft voice and warm smile. It was like God placed an angel right there in the form of a secretary. She was the one who helped me fill out all of the paperwork. The certification would cost me five thousand dollars. We all know this girl didn't have that kind of money, so I had to fill out paperwork for all of the school grants. I had absolutely no clue where to begin, but Julie helped me. School started two weeks from that first meeting, and I began to question if I was really ready. Was I ready for this at all? Was I ready to change my life forever? I didn't actually know the answer at the time, but I just kept taking the next step and it all started to fall into place. I lived thirty minutes away from the school, which made it a little difficult to go back and forth between school and my waitressing gig. A few nights a week, I would just sleep in my car, pull clothes out of my trunk, and go into class. I bet I smelled really good...

I had started seeing my son, Ozzie, some, but it was limited because of all I had been through and put him through. I actually got fired from my job as a waitress because I still had partying issues. But God works it all out, because a girl that was in school with me actually helped me get a job where she worked, at a restaurant called The Fisherman's Warf. It was a cute seafood restaurant and it would change my life forever. The fact that I had a job brought me a little hope, because I had one hard blow after another with my previous jobs. So, with this new job and being in beauty school, things were looking up.

I filled out paper work to get government assistance with my living and childcare, because at this point, I was going to be getting Ozzie for two weeks on and two weeks off. This was an amazing thing, but there was a waiting list for the housing and childcare help. I still just kept doing the next right thing the best way I knew how. Clubbing and going out still had a strong hold on me for a while. I was going out a lot and sleeping around, but I thought it was progress that I wasn't sleeping around to get high.

I met this guy who was in a band. He said that he was a Christian, but he didn't really act any different than any other man I went out with, if you get what I am saying. While dating him, I got the call that a house was ready for me to move into. Wow, a house! I would have a room for my son to sleep in, and I wouldn't have to crash on people's couches or sleep in my car anymore. I was beginning to see blessing over my life. Dating this guy, though he didn't always act like a Christian, did make me more curious about the Bible and Christian music. Here is another word picture for you: I would read the Bible while having a cigarette hanging out of my mouth, and letting the ashes fall onto the pages. I would also read the church marquee signs around town. I always felt like the words on those signs were straight from God and directly for me.

FEED YOUR FAITH AND YOUR DOUBT WILL STARVE.

I would see this right when I was doubting something.

YOU MAKE THE CHOICE AND GOD MAKES THE CHANGE.

This would come when I was questioning if He could change me.

TRADE GOD YOUR PIECES FOR HIS PEACE.

Was it really possible for me to have peace?

Nonetheless, I honestly thought this guy was my knight in shining armor and that we were going to live happily ever after. He was great with my son and had a great family, but I was still a hot mess and didn't care about anyone but myself. So, I would go on meth binges. I would cheat on him, and eventually he couldn't take it anymore and left. It broke my heart, y'all. I hit the pavement hard. Everything that had ever hurt me came rushing back. Even though I had gotten government housing and was living on my own. Even though I had a job and was halfway through beauty school. I thought this breakup was going to be what killed me. I wanted to die again. My heart hurt so badly. It wasn't necessarily the breakup, it was more that I screwed up every good thing that came my way. I believed this guy was a huge blessing in my life, but when I look back now, he definitely wasn't the man God had for me. But, at the time, thoughts of suicide began to flood back in. I thought, *"My life is not worth fighting for. It is always going to be hard. I am never going to change or find happiness. God can't help me. I am a hopeless cause. Just end it all, Jessica."* Then I heard a noise on my back porch. I thought someone was trying to break in. It got my focus off trying to kill myself for a minute, so I called my friend Ackdog and asked him to come over to check. Now I think it was a hallucination. I think I was wanting it to be someone there to kill me. God works in mysterious ways. This saved me for the night, because when my friend got to my house, he saw the wreck that I was and decided to sit with me until I fell asleep. Here is another scripture that spoke directly to this moment in my life.

Psalm 30:5 NIV- For his anger lasts only a moment, but his favor lasts a lifetime; weeping may stay for the night, but rejoicing comes in the morning.

That is exactly what happened that night. Before falling asleep, I wanted to end it all. When I woke up, my grit was back. My fight. I may not have seen my life put back together in my mind, but that didn't stop me from believing that it could be. But, just know, that when your fight comes back, so does the devil. He comes to attack our worth and value every time.

I had gotten into some money trouble and needed extra cash. There was this guy that used to come into the General Store that I worked at when I was sixteen. He would offer me the world. He was a rich business man from Dallas who had a wife, but wanted me at all costs. I may have been a little slutty at the time, but I was not a prostitute and I wasn't about to have a "sugar daddy." Fast forward from sixteen to now, through a whole lot of brokenness, and there he sat one night at the bar where I worked. *Why now?! Why would this temptation walk in when I need cash?!* Because that is how the devil works. If you haven't figured it out in your life yet, I hope this helps you. The devil will bait you with the one thing you need at the exact moment that you need it, just so he can continue to ruin your life. I don't remember the first thing he said to me when he saw me, but I clearly remember these words, "My offer still stands. Let me take care of you, so you never have to worry about money again." Me, never having to worry about money again? He said, "I will give you one thousand dollars to meet me at the Arlington Resort Hotel." A thousand dollars would pay my lawyer fees so that I could get my son back. That is when I began to convince myself that this was harmless and that I needed to do it. I mean, I wouldn't be doing anything that I didn't do most every other night with different men. This time it would be better because I would be getting paid, and this would help me advance my life. This guy's timing couldn't have been better, so I convinced myself that this was the way it was supposed to happen. This was how I was always going to be taken care of. *Sex was all my body was worth anyway, so why not do it right and get some money for it?* What the hell was I thinking? The present Jessica is now screaming at past Jessica, saying, "No, it's a trap! It's a detour! It is a distraction from where you are going! Don't do it!" Unfortunately, it doesn't work that way. I don't know that it would have been of any use anyway, because that Jessica was selfish and prideful. And yet there is another scripture that speaks to who that girl was.

Proverbs 16:18 NLT- Pride goes before destruction and haughtiness before a fall.

I would have been too prideful to listen to anyone before I walked into that hotel room. So, I did what I never thought I would do. I went to that hotel room and I fell again. This fall was different. The pain was different. He gave me the money, but he took what pride I had left in myself. The pride of never messing with another woman's husband. Before, I was knew I was bad, but I wasn't a homewrecker. Now I was.

Spoiler alert! This moment happened only three months before God radically changed my life. I had no clue what was about to happen. I was at the bottom of this pit emotionally, physically, and mentally. But, God knew even that night in the hotel room that in a few short months, He would be sending someone who would show me who He was. I say all of this to say: your victory is closer than you think! Freedom is right around the corner! So, don't give up when life looks the most hopeless. Keep getting back up!

Ten

BECOMING MRS. YOUNGBLOOD
PART I

Jesus came and sat in my section one night while at work. He came in the form of a man. This man would be who God used to restore what other men had done to break me.

One night I went to work at Fisherman's Warf. There were two guys that would come in every night to eat and drink. One of the guys had dated a few of the girls that I worked with and the other was a well-known drug dealer in town. For obvious reasons I didn't want anything to do with them, so I never looked at their table or wanted to wait on them. This one particular night, I had no choice. They sat at the hottest table in my section. When I realized that there was no way to avoid them, I went to my manager and asked if someone else could take the table, but he said no. I was pissed because it was as if everyone wanted me to fail. Didn't they know I was trying to get sober? Didn't they know I wasn't a strong person and this would make me stumble? But, I had no choice, so I got my notepad and took their orders. I started by saying, "What do y'all want?" Trey, the drug dealer, started to say something about God leading and following me. Honestly, I was half-way listening because I didn't understand why a guy like him would be talking to me about God. Who did he think he was? So, that made me even madder. I was searching for hope and this guy was trying to talk to me about the Savior of the World? I just walked away and got their Coors Lights. I brought them back and slammed them on the table and asked what they wanted to eat. That is when it happened. That is the moment that forever changed my life. Trey said, "Would you want to go out with me sometime?" I gave him the "you can't be serious/go to hell" look and said, "No, but I will go out with your friend." I hadn't even really looked at his face until that moment and I glanced over and saw perfect eyebrows, slick hair, and a soft sweet smile. My first thought was, *"Okay, I guess that didn't go too badly. At least he isn't ugly."* That put a crack in the wall I had built up and I got "unmad" about them being at my table. We started talking about the local car dealership where they worked and other random things. Eventually, I laid the check on the table and said, "I'll take care of this when you are ready." They paid and they left. So, to see if Trey's friend knew I was serious, I called the dealership the next day to talk to Trey. I asked him what his friend said and wondered if he knew that I was serious when I asked him out.

So, who was his friend and what was he like? I didn't know and I didn't care. I would date anyone and everyone that seemed like a good time and if he was hanging out with Trey, I was sure that he would be fun. I eventually found out his name: Jonathan Youngblood. I was a pretty blunt girl who did what she had to do to keep from losing, so the next day I called their work and talked to Jon. I said, "I thought we were going out." I guess he was scared to say no, so he said, "Okay."

Before we ever even went on our first date, I asked him to bring me gum so I could see him. He brought the gum to my nasty crackhouse. It was so bad, it literally smelled like pee. I was wearing booty shorts and my thong was showing at the top. And to top off the outfit, I had a doo-rag on. Oh, and I think I forgot to mention, I actually had a guy I was messing around with at the time. But as you have come to know, there was always something or someone "new" coming along that I would have to sleep with or hang out with, and I'd leave the "old" hanging. I told Jon on the phone before he came over that I would have to break up with my boyfriend. When he showed up with the gum, I tried to kiss him immediately because that is all I knew how to do with boys. He pulled away and said, "No way! Did you take care of that boyfriend situation?" I hadn't yet, but I dumped the guy very quickly after that, because I wanted this new guy.

He had it all: the look, a good job, and a nice truck. I just knew that everyone would be jealous of me. You know the qualifications to be my boyfriend at this time weren't anything special because I was still clubbing and drinking a lot. I was most excited to have sex with him on our first date. I even told all of the girls at beauty school that I had found my husband. Which, truth be told, wasn't anything new for them to hear because I was "in love with" and planned to marry anyone I dated. Remember, I wanted to be rescued. I wanted a man to come and sweep me off my feet like in the movies. I think if we are honest, this describes a lot of us. How many people have you said that you loved who didn't turn out to be your husband or wife? Exactly. Anyway, our first date was at Popeyes Chicken. I guess that is what he thought I was worth. He had two roommates at the time. The drug dealer, Trey, and another guy named Gabe. They were both super nice guys, but even then, Jon was different. Yes, he drank, but he didn't act crazy. He didn't do drugs or smoke. Unlike me, who smoked a lot. We started dating, and of course, I got him to sleep with me pretty quickly. I thought that was love, and I thought that was how you kept a man. It was a way for me to maintain control of their emotions. *If I sleep with them and keep them happy, they won't leave me* (until I find another guy at least). I kept feeling like Jon wasn't falling for my usual spell. He was having fun, but wasn't falling for me with his heart. An internal part of me panicked like, "Wait, I can't hurt him… that means it is not like the others." It freaked me out, but I was still very much into him, so we kept seeing each other.

About three weeks into dating, we had a Christmas party at work and I asked Jon to be my date. I was excited to go because there would be free drinks all night! To no one's surprise, I got hammered. I started talking really vulgarly to everyone, making a scene and a fool of myself. The things that were coming out of my mouth you wouldn't hear in a men's locker room. We all had to bring a gift, and I definitely brought my gift. Let's just say, you can't buy it at Walmart and it was a fruit that took batteries. After seeing the hot mess that I was that night, Jon tried to break up with me. He said, "You aren't the type of woman that I see myself being with." *Excuse me? What?* I was in shock.

I hadn't heard those words since I lost my virginity, and even then it wasn't the guy breaking up with me, it was just his pregnant girlfriend screaming at me. Then I said (in a very country, ghetto way), "Oh no you ain't, boy! You ain't breaking up with me!" I asked him, "What kind of woman do you want? Teach me how to be her."

He started to tell me about his upbringing. He grew up in a Christian home with amazing parents who loved God. The season of life that he was in was the first time he had ever drank, much less dated someone like me. He began to tell me about the life he saw for himself and that it would start with him going back to church. I was all in. I was all in because I had had always wanted to be someone different, but I didn't know how to get there. I didn't know how to be the girl he talked about. I was ready to do whatever it took. I did try to tell him about my life, in a sad, "pity me" type of way, and he was the first person not to fall for it. He was the first person who ever told me that I needed to get over my past and move forward with what God had for me.

All my life I had let my past create who I was, and I had never been around anyone who wanted more for themselves. What is so sad is that God had Jon planned all along for me. This amazing Christian man. What had I been doing to prepare for such a guy? Nothing! The saddest part of my story, and the only thing I regret (because I don't regret much, hence the book title) was having to tell this man about my past and having to tell him that I had given all of myself away to anyone who would give me the time of day. The heartbreak that filled his eyes is something I will never forget. But, he saw the desperation in my eyes that screamed for change. He could see that I was desperate to be more than I was. So, we started going to church. Don't get it twisted just yet; we did still live in sin, and by that I mean having sex while unmarried. But, the way he looked at me, the way he talked to me, and the way he treated me was so beautiful. So, in January of 2003, I went to meet Jon's family for the first time, and I took Ozzie with me. I had no idea how this family would take me. I mean, I had a son named Ozzie for crying out loud. I was definitely still rough around the edges. I didn't know if they would think I was good enough. I don't really even remember now how that night went.

I just remember this perfect looking family, all proper and classy, getting some play dough from our waiter and playing with Ozzie. Just like that, they accepted him. I had such a hard shell, I could deal with not being liked, but I wanted them to like my son. If you liked my son, I was happy. So, here I was, finishing beauty school, feeling in love, and knowing he was going to be my husband. Do you want to know how I knew this? Because for the first time ever in my whole life, I didn't want to ruin it. I didn't want to run out and sleep with anyone else. I wanted a family like the one I saw at that table at On the Border, the family that he grew up with. The question was, could I have that? Could a girl like me really transform and become a beautiful, loving wife?

In February, Jon was able to talk me into going to his parents' house for the weekend. Y'all, their house was like a home from a magazine, so clean and so perfect. There was something expensive in every corner. They told me I would be sleeping on the pull-out bed in the music room. I had no problem with that. Before dinner that night, I was sitting at the kitchen island, talking to Jon's mom, and out came my whole life story. Where I had been, what I had done, how I was lost, but finding my way. Looking back now, knowing the amazing Christian woman that she is, I am surprised she didn't have a heart attack right then and there. But, she just listened to me very intently, and then I always imagine she went straight to her room and hit her knees for the girl that her son had just brought home. Y'all know I still wasn't the girl that you would bring home to momma. Even still, that night, in that music room, I felt God tugging on my heart. I felt love wrap around my body. I looked up to the gold chandelier and told God that I wanted this to be my life, and that I wanted to be the person that He had called me to be. I surrendered my whole life to him that night. I said, "I give you my past and my future. Show me the steps. I want to be transformed." I wanted it so badly, and I knew Jon was who God had used to bring me there. Hear this loud and clear: Jon was not the one that saved me. He is just the one who brought me to the feet of Jesus. Jesus is the only person that truly saves; He just works through random people in random ways. So, God used Jon to chisel away my rough edges, and helped me give up the things that were not pointing me back to Jesus and who He had called me to be. I felt such a sense of becoming greater. And yet, because God's ways are higher than our ways, and His thoughts are higher than our thoughts, I had no idea what He had in store. Blessing after blessing began to pour in, and I was just in awe. Jon and I had looked at wedding rings, which was so exciting. Then, I got an upgrade in my government living situation and Jon started "staying on the couch." No, we didn't do everything perfectly. I could feel your judgement jumping off the page for the couch situation (ha!)! We were just trying to find our way. This home was the most amazing thing that I had ever had. I remember listening to Christian music and doing the dishes one day. I was taking pride in what God had given me. Before Jon, I had a mattress on the floor, but then his parents bought me a real fancy bed. Guys, when I talk about God putting back together every broken thing, this is what I am talking about. If we open our eyes and see that He is the one providing for us, we can be thankful for it all and it changes our perspective!

PART II

The day came when Jon was going to propose. I wasn't a girl who had dreamed of being proposed to, or had a vision of the proposal. But honestly, if I had one, my vision would have been better than it actually went. He told me that day to make reservations for a nice dinner. I had changed, but I hadn't changed that much yet. I hadn't made nice dinner reservations before. I guess I said something in the car that alerted him to the fact that I knew he was about to propose. The next thing I know, he tossed the ring in my lap and said, "I got you something." In my head I was like, *"Uhhhh, I guess tonight isn't the night because who throws an engagement ring into the lap of his future wife?"* Well folks, Jon did. I laugh thinking back on this. I opened the box and was shocked. It was perfect. It was breathtaking. How could this be real? Was this my Cinderella moment? Was I going to actually have a fairytale ending to a horrible beginning? Would I be chosen to be loved by a man that I trusted? Would God give me a man that was so pure until meeting me? Would God give me a man that would forget my past? Did God give me this amazing man to be a father to my Ozzie? Yes! A thousand times, yes! Y'all, God has more for us than we could ever dream, think, or imagine!

Ephesians 3:20 MSG- God can do anything, you know- far more than you could ever imagine, guess, or request in your wildest dreams! He does it not by using us around, but by working within us, His spirit deeply and gently within us.

If you need physical proof that the Scripture is alive and well today, just look at my life. Ephesians 3:20 was my life! It still is my life!

The Youngblood family accepted me, and it was crazy how God already had things planned. I firmly believe that I did not die because of my mother-in-law's prayers. She spent her whole life praying for her children and their future spouses. What she didn't know when she was praying those prayers is that her future daughter-in-law, the wife of her first born son, was fighting to live. How amazing is that? Beyond her prayers, she became the missing link of my childhood; a mother. She stepped up and was the mother that my own was not. During wedding season she took me dress shopping, helped me pick out my jewelry, and all the things that mothers do. It was truly special. Months went by and we filled up every detail in our wedding book. My dad still didn't make a lot of money, so my in-laws ended up paying for the wedding of my dreams (really, the wedding that I would have dreamed up if I was the dreaming kind back then). I never truly thought this would happen for me, but August 15, 2003 came, the day before the wedding. My dress was fitted, the tuxedos were in, and rehearsal was happening. In that moment, I lost it. The eight months prior to that night had gone so fast. I realized as I was standing there that I was a walking miracle. I knew right then that I would be telling the goodness of God for the rest of my life.

As the next day came, I got up and put on my white dress, because y'all, God makes all things new! Pure was never a word that I had been called, but Jon and I tried to straighten up our act and stopped sleeping with each other a few months before the wedding. I'm sure we had a few slip ups, but we would get up again every day and try to not give up. Thankfully, just like God makes all things new, His mercies are new every morning, too. So, the day had come and my dad arrived with a clean-shaven face and red puffy eyes. The man had already been crying. I know they were tears of joy. I know he had flashbacks to the time when I was lying in bed, half dead, detoxing from meth, and then thinking on the day that we were in. He knew I had found the man that would love me for the rest of my life. I also think that he knew in his heart that once I was married, my life wouldn't end up with divorce like his did. He was a proud papa that day. As for me, I was actually not an emotional wreck. Thankfully, I had gotten all of that out the day before. I looked around in complete awe. God gave this daughter, His daughter, her Cinderella moment. I was thankful for the beautiful fire and ice roses, the fancy food, and the freaking ice sculptures that I had only ever seen in pictures. I was thankful to have an amazing daddy to walk me down the aisle to an amazing man who would take my hand at the end. "I now pronounce you husband and wife" is all I heard the officiant say, or at least is all I remember from the day. We were Mr. & Mrs. Youngblood. Wow.

The perfect day passed and I still had a long way to go in my transformation. My mother-in-law knew it, too. She had read a book by Joyce Meyer and knew that it would help me. It was this black and blue book with chess pieces on the cover, and it was called, *"Battlefield of the Mind."* The title alone drew me in, because my mind had always been a battlefield. In bold letters on the back of the book it said, "There's a war going on and your mind is the battlefield." So, I knew it was time to put in the work. You have to do the work after the honeymoon is over. Sadly, that is what the world keeps forgetting.

So, when you find hope and let light peek through to the bottom of your pit, when you feel like you can breathe a little easier, when you feel like your life may be different than everyone around you, remember this scripture:

Matthew 14:27 NIV - But Jesus immediately said to them, "Take courage! It is I. Don't be afraid."

I felt like I finally heard this from Jesus. I had been with many men, and Jesus was not with them (quite the opposite, actually). But this time was different. Jesus was with Jon. I would become the "Mrs." that Jon deserved, and taking his last name would give me a fresh start. In the Bible God turned water into wine, and in my life he turned a ho into a housewife.

Eleven

TRANSFORMATION
PART I

When I was younger, we actually did go to church. We were that "go once a year so you could say that you went and check it off your list" type. We had a little church in Daisy, Arkansas that I loved. The pastors there were amazing. They loved me and welcomed me in when I had alcohol on my breath and my clothes smelled like I smoked in the car with the windows up (which I did). I would go in there and hear the pastor preach, though I didn't know what he was saying. I only remember when he talked about coming forward and accepting Christ as my Savior, and recognizing all He had done for me. What my mind heard him say was, "If you get up and walk down the aisle with your scarlet stains, everything will be fixed." So, I did that again and again. I even got baptized hoping that it would change me. Of course, it didn't. I would leave the church and think back to all the people sitting in the pews and how Jesus worked for them; but none of them were as bad off as me, so He couldn't save me. Every time I would get to the bottom of that rope, I would try the church thing again. And every time I would be sad again because I just didn't think walking down the aisle was for me. How many of us do this every Sunday and still don't find hope? Still walking around as hopeless as we were, or even more so, because the One everyone says saves the world isn't saving you. You probably can't get rid of the thoughts that plague your mind. Thoughts about everything getting better if you just end your life, because the pain of living is too much to bear another day. Let me tell you, you are not alone! That is why this chapter exists. I wanted to bring you some insight of why this happens to so many people. Getting saved isn't going to transform you. I wanted to get saved to relieve my pain. I wanted a miracle potion that would touch me once and I would be free. But, that is not the case. It is not going to fix all of your mess. That is hopeless Christianity.

The hope that God offers is what fixes you. Getting saved is just the beginning. It's like the batter's box. You make a choice to be on the team, you get in the warm up circle, and you are the next batter up. If you stay in the batter's box and never actually swing, you never experience what it's actually like to play the game. Getting saved is so much like that. We all want to sit on the sidelines and yell at what God should do, but we never actually do anything to change ourselves. A life transformed is a life surrendered. You can't party all week then show up to church and think that is going to work. To put it nicely, you are putting a sprinkle of God on your worldly cupcake and expecting a change. It is not going to work. For me, meeting and marrying Jon is where I started doing the work that it took to be all that God created me to be.

You already know that I really hated school. I never read books that I didn't have to for an assignment. The book my mother-in-law gave me, *Battlefield of the Mind*, would be the first book I ever sat down and read on my own. I read the first chapter and couldn't stop. The author, Joyce, was speaking straight to my heart and whole life. Everything she said was so true. It showed me that my thoughts created so many of the problems in my life. It taught me how to change and create new thoughts. I knew if Joyce could overcome what she had gone through and live a good life, I could too.

Finally, I knew this Christian stuff was real. It was like chips and salsa; I could not stop. I was hungry for more. I wanted to be something more in this life. To become the woman God had purposed for me to become. So, I started applying the principle that I was learning from the book and the scriptures that it referenced. Let me be real for a minute. When you are a new Christian, the Bible thing is scary. Somehow, that didn't apply to me. When I looked at the scriptures, it was like God's letter made just for me, his daughter. I was going to be taking my beauty school boards that spring, I had married this perfect man, and I was sober. I was full of happiness. We all have that moment where our past will try to creep in again and will try to make us push away the people we love. Jon never would have that, though. He wouldn't let me wallow in my self-pity. He would tell me that I needed to get over it. He would always say, "If you are going to become something new, you have to stop thinking and living like the old." So, that told me that I would have to get out of Hot Springs and cut ties with all of my rowdy friends. I would have to stop doing what I had always done.

The time came, and thank the Lord, I passed my cosmetology boards. I was going to be a hairstylist! My first job was with Smart Style (you know, the salons in WalMart). I wasn't very good, so I didn't want to go anywhere that I could mess with someone's brand or reputation. We eventually left Hot Springs and moved to Texarkana, to a house that Jon's parents bought and we rented. Jon was working with his dad and making about $2,000 a month. That was a lot of money to us. I didn't want to work at just any salon, so I started waiting tables until I could get used to the new city. Before Jon and I got married, I remember my mother-in-law taking me to get my hair done for one of our wedding showers and I was chatting with the hairstylist, Leslie. She and her husband, Danny, owned the salon. They didn't just hire people. They hired them and trained them. That is what I wanted! I wanted to learn. So, they hired me and I began to work for them on salary for six months. I was beyond happy to be there.

We went to the Baptist Church that Jon's parents went to. I had to get some appropriate dresses to wear, although at the time I referred to them as "grandma dresses." Being a new Christian, I felt like I had to look like everyone else. I was reading anything I could get my hands on and watching anything that would tell me more about God. I was even going to Christian concerts. I was on fire. When I began my walk with God, I knew that I was going to do great things and help pull people from the same pit I was in for so long. Six months into our marriage and my new found faith, we found out that we were expecting. We were having another little boy. He came and we named him Ezra. He was a great baby. But, having a baby always exposes cracks in your marriage and in your relationships. The way I mothered looked so different than the way Jon was mothered. That isn't to say one way is better than another, but it can create tension. As soon as Ezra was six weeks old, I had to go back to work. I loved my job at the salon and I actually had great clientele at this point. My success in cosmetology became my identity. Being a mom wasn't as easy for me.

We still lived in our three-bed, one-bath home, and our little family was making it work. I was trying to work full time, still grow in my transformation, and be the wife I had never seen before. Can I just tell you, if you want to be something different than what you know, then you need to surround yourself with people who have wisdom and experience and who read books. That's what I did. Slowly but surely things got easier in our marriage, while also being a full time working mom. Ozzie would still come visit every other weekend, so that would change our family dynamic for a short period, but we learned to adapt. But, I still had a complex of feeling "less than." It all came to a head when Jon got a new job making great money and I was making great money. We began to buy things. A lot of things. This mostly speaks to me, but when you grow up without and then find yourself in a place where you have the means to buy things you couldn't have, you go crazy. I didn't know how to find a good balance. It was from one extreme to another. I had nothing and then I had it all. At the time I called it "being blessed." That is a hardcore lie! Using a credit card isn't called being blessed, it is called debt, and it is the devil's playground. And what happens next? We found out that we were pregnant again. So, I was now off work for maternity leave, Jon's job was crumbling, and we realized ($30,000 later) that we should have been saving for a rainy day. We had nothing to really show for all of our hard work. You can't spend beyond your means because if the means stop the bills keeps coming, and with the bills come major stress.

Our second kid, another boy, was here and we named him Zeeland. He was a difficult one. He cried a lot and required a lot of attention. So, we brought him home to a house that we could no longer afford, and we were stressed to the max with Jon's job situation. Truth be told, in these times, I did have a sense of peace. I knew that God would bring us through it. After all, I had been telling women who sat in my chair about all the great things God had done and the situations He brought me out of. So, I had to know that He would do the same again, even if our debt was totally our fault. So, in this season, we started trusting God in new ways. Jon's parents actually bailed us out, but our habits didn't change. We talked a good game, but our spending was the same. This would catch up with us down the road, but for now, we were good again. So, we sold our house on Westline Court and bought another on Desoto Drive. This house was even more perfect. It had a huge backyard with the most perfect Magnolia tree. I looked around and thought, "I can raise my boys here forever."

PART II

The Lord took away all of my addictions (smoking, drinking, using meth, pornography, and sleeping around) when I surrendered them to him. To surrender them to Him is to give them all to Him. Let go of the grip you have on them and let go of the shame and guilt that has its grip on you. With surrender comes work, so I had to do the work to transform. If you don't know by now, the point of this book is to give you hope. Finding Jesus is finding hope, but I do have some practical things that can help in getting out of your pit. So, now it's your turn to do some work to transform into the person God has called you to be.

I know parts of my story can look glamorous and you may be thinking, "I don't have a Jon in my life to support me or guide me to change." Well, that is the first perspective that needs to change. That mentality needs to shift right now. Let me just tell you, it won't do you a bit of good to have a Jon in your life to walk you through the steps if you aren't desperate enough to know you need a Savior, and that Jesus Christ is that Savior. If you continue to sit on your high horse of pride, then you will be sitting on an excuse not to change. But, if you are ready and you are asking, then the rest of this book will help you.

Let's word picture for a minute: changing is kind of like the process of having your hair colored. It starts with the application of bleach, stripping your hair down, filling it with the color, and then cleansing it. Once you wash it, it is renewed. It is different. That is exactly what we have to do with our lives and minds. You can get saved all day long, but if you don't renew your thought life, you will stay just the way you are. So, we are going to break down the hair coloring process into four steps: Application, Stripping Away, Filling, and Cleansing.

1. Application

The bottom line is you have to apply God's word to your life. It is alive and active and applying it to your life has the power to mold you into a different human. When you are so hungry for what God says about you, it becomes louder than all of the other voices in your head. But (because there is always a "but"), you can't just read the Bible. No, you have to apply the principles and promises that it teaches. We can't just read the Bible like it is another Twilight sequel. We have to read it and listen to what God is speaking to us through His Holy Spirit. It takes a lot of faith. I have heard people say that becoming a Christian is weak and they don't need it, but if you watch the news for even five minutes you will see that our world is in a war between good and evil. Sin has taken over this world and it is so unpredictable. One day you have a man shooting up a concert and another day there is a man plowing his truck through a group of bikers. Everything that is happening in our world could make you feel like there is no hope, but when you have God's word in your heart, it fills you with hope to know that the battle has already been won. Jesus won the ultimate battle when He died on the cross. So, if you are in denial that there is evil in this world, you should just put this book down. Admitting we are enslaved in sin is the only way you will ever want to apply God's grace to your life. When we drop our pride and admit that we need a Savior, He is there waiting with open arms. And the beautiful thing is, we don't have to clean up first. He wants us to come as we are and then He will wash us clean with His saving grace, perfect love, and unfailing hope.

Romans 10:9-10 NLT- If you openly declare that Jesus is Lord and believe in your heart that God raised him from the dead, you will be saved. For it is by believing in your heart that you are made right with God, and it is by openly declaring your faith that you are saved.

Romans 6:16 NLT- Don't you realize that you become the slave of whatever you choose to obey? You can be a slave to sin, which leads to death, or you can choose to obey God, which leads to righteous living.

2. Strip Away the Old

We have to surrender it all. Once we admit we are sinners and that we need Jesus, we go through a stripping process. God is going to ask you to let go of the things that the world loves. The things that you love. Some things He may ask us to let go of can even be good things that we have that have been thrown out of balance. He will only ask us to let go of them for a season. That means we won't have to let go of some things forever, but for a period of time. He truly has everything worked out in His perfect timing. You may not understand why He is asking it of you at the time, but down the road, you will know and it will all make sense. This process is very important to your end result. Trust me, if you try to hang onto anything in your old life, it will leave a stink on your new life. You have to trust God completely in this process. You have to let Him wash away all of the scarlet stains of your sinful life. If I were to just put the purple color on top of my dark hair without stripping it first, the purple would never show up. I have to strip away the old color to make room for the new. Your soul is the same. You have to strip away the old to transform into the new. You have to strip away your selfish desires! "Selfish" can seem like a harsh word, but it is true and applicable to all of our lives. We all have selfish ways, we just have to recognize them and run the opposite direction of where they are calling. I know you may feel as if you won't make it through the pain of losing something, but hold on tight, because something better is coming in to fill your life and make you happier than you could ever imagine. You have never known true peace until you strip away the old and make room for Jesus.

Ephesians 4:22 NLT - Throw off your old sinful nature and your former way of life, which is corrupted by lust and deception.

3. The Filling

If you just go through the stripping process, you will not be complete. You will be left feeling empty and wondering what the purpose was in stripping it all away. So, don't stop there. As a colorist, if I just applied the bleach and stripped away the old, it looks like I don't know what I am doing and like I am not victorious in my coloring technique. That is how so many Christians look. They get saved and they quit smoking, drinking, or whatever it is in their life that they needed to let go of, but they don't enter into an actual relationship with Jesus. Then they wonder why it isn't working and why it feels so hard to maintain that life. You can't start or maintain anything in your own power. You and I are not strong enough to kick drugs, pre-marital sex, or anything else on our own. We have to enter into a relationship with Jesus and He will guide us, give us the strength, and make a way when it doesn't look like there is one.

Galatians 5:16-23 MSG (Written by the Apostle Paul)

My counsel is this: Live freely, animated, and motived by God's spirit. Then you won't feed the compulsions of selfishness. For there is a root of sinful self-interest in us that is at odds with a free spirit, just as the free spirit is incompatible with selfishness. These two ways of life are antithetical, so that you cannot lives at times one way and at times another way according to how you feel on any given day. Why don't you choose to be led by the Spirit and so escape the erratic compulsion of a law-dominated existence? It is obvious what kind of life develops out of trying to get your own way all of the time: repetitive loveless, cheap sex; an accumulation of mental and emotional garbage; frenzied and joyless grabs for happiness; trinket gods; magic-show religion; paranoid loneliness; cutthroat competition; all-consuming-yet-never-satisfied wants; a brutal temper; an impotence to love or be loved; divided homes and divided lives; small minded and lopsided pursuits; the vicious habit of depersonalizing everyone into a rival; uncontrolled and uncontrollable addictions; ugly parodies of community. I could go on. But, this isn't the first time I have warned you, you know. If you use your freedom this way, you will not inherit God's kingdom. But what happens when we live God's way? He brings gifts into our lives, much the same way the fruit appears in an orchard- things like affection for others, exuberance about life, serenity. We develop a willingness to stick with things, a sense of compassion in the heart, and a conviction that is basic holiness permeates things and people. We find ourselves involved in loyal commitments, not needing to force our way into life, able to marshal and direct our energies wisely.

Philippians 4:8-9 NLT- "Fix your thoughts on what is true and honorable, and right, and pure, and lovely and admirable. Think about things that are excellent and worthy of praise. Keep putting into practice all you learned and received from me. Everything you heard from me and saw me doing. Then the God of peace will be with you."

Ephesians 4:23-24 NLT- Let the spirit renew your thoughts and attitudes. Put on your new nature, created to be like God, truly righteous and holy.

4. Cleansing

When you're living a life of sin, some crap gets on you. You become stained with guilt and shame. You are bombarded with the memories of your past and you carry them everywhere you go, but the Lord says He makes us white as snow. While God is in the business of cleansing our past and making us new, there will still be consequences from our past choices. For example, my son Ozzie, still to this day, lives with his dad because of the choice I made to follow meth and give up my custody when he was a baby. That doesn't mean God didn't wipe my past clean, there are just effects that I still have to live with. Your life isn't going to be perfect. To relate this back to the hair coloring process, on your first wash you will see a lot of purple water flowing away, and while your hair looks great, you will still see color washing away for many shampoos to come! So, let God wash over you every day. Let His word and his spirit flow over your heart and mind every day. You don't just take a shower once in your life and expect to stay clean forever. Yes, Jesus washes away your sins when you accept His salvation, but you have to keeping taking a shower in His word to keep a clean heart and mind.

Isaiah 1:18 NLT- "Come now, let's settle this," says, The Lord. "Though your sins are like scarlet,
I will make them as white as snow; though they are red as crimson, they shall be like wool."

Psalm 32:1-7 NIV- Blessed is the one whose transgressions are forgiven, whose sins are covered.
Blessed is the one who sin the Lord does not count against them and in whose spirit is no deceit.
When I kept silent, my bones wasted away through my growing all day long. For day and night your
hand was heavy on me; my strength was sapped as in the heat of the summer. Then I acknowledged
my sin to you and did not cover up my iniquity. I said, "I will confess my transgressions to the Lord."
And you forgave the guilt of my sin.

When you are renewed you feel alive! You glow and have a light about you that people are drawn to. They want to know what it is! And that, my friends, that is where it gets good.

2 Corinthians 5:17-18 NLT- Anyone who belongs to Christ has become a new person. The old life
is gone; and a new life has begun. And all this is a gift from God, who brought us back to himself
through Christ. And God has given us this task of reconciling people to Him.

This is what it is all about. Living a victorious Christian life and having a daily relationship with Christ draws people to us, and that's where we then point them to Jesus. We can share what we have found in Him and in His word. Again, just like my purple hair, everywhere I go people stop me and ask, "Where did you get that done?" Or they say, "I love your hair, I wish I could wear that!" That happens to Christians who shine with Jesus. People ask them, "What is different about you? Why are you so happy? Where is this light from? I wish I could be happy and peaceful like you." Well, you can! God is not a respecter of persons. He wants all of us!

Romans 2:11 NLT- For God does not show favoritism.

We can have a full, abundant life. No matter who we are or where we are at!

John 10:10 NIV- "*The thief comes only to steal and kill and destroy; I have come that they may have life, and have it to the full!*"

But, don't get caught in the trap of comparison. Don't look at someone else's life and want what they have. Create the life you want to have by starting today in your transformation process!

Twelve

FORGIVENESS
PART I

Isaiah 61:3 NLT - To all who mourn in Israel, he will give a crown of beauty for ashes, a joyous blessing instead of mourning, festive praise instead of despair, they will be like great oaks that the Lord has planted for his own Glory.

There comes a time in our lives when we wake up one day and face the truth of where our life has ended up. We wonder how we got there and how we can change it. The truth is the only thing that can set us free. Something starts burning so strongly, deep inside of your soul, that says your life has to be more than what it is right now. You and I can't always have this hate in our heart, and we can't carry this shame and guilt forever. For me, I started thinking, *"Can my life be different than my family's life has been for generations? Could I break the cycle of a mother that abandons her children, just as my mother had done to me, and her mother to her?"* Being abandoned at 8 months old creates scars. With me, the scars were so deep that it took years to get over them, and it affected every area in my life. It affected how I thought teachers felt about me. I thought everyone who entered my life would leave me. I would give any boy who showed me attention whatever he wanted, hoping he wouldn't abandon me too. That all led me straight to my meth addiction that almost killed me. The chain reaction of abandonment is undeniable and will continue until someone finds freedom from their past and stops the cycle. So, with my transformation process underway, I then had to begin the journey to find healing and forgiveness toward the ones who hurt me most. I finally learned how to forgive myself for all the choices I made while in pain. I believed, as shattered as my life was, surely God's word was true and He could make something beautiful out of my ashes.

And y'all, He did. That's what He wants to do in your life; He will give you beauty for ashes.

I knew the road to freedom wasn't going to be easy. With a past like mine and everything I had endured, I had to surrender my life to him daily. But, I was willing to do whatever I had to do to get out of my misery and not cause pain to my children. It was because I let the "old Jessica" die, so that I could become a new creation in Christ. Remember, I had to strip off everything that hindered me to become new. And one of the biggest hindrances in moving forward is being unable to forgive.

Hebrews 12:1 NIV - Therefore, since we are surrounded by such a great cloud of witnesses, let us throw off everything that hinders and the sin that so easily entangles. And let us run with perseverance the race marked out for us.

You don't run a race with baggage. You don't run a race backwards. You run it forward with as little extra weight as possible. Why? Because it helps you run forward faster. If we continuously look into our past and carry around the sin or the hurt people have done to us, it will stop us from fulfilling our true purpose. God can't turn the ashes into something beautiful if we don't give him the ashes. You have to renew your mind and change your thought patterns. What you think in your mind is what controls you.

Romans 12:2 NLT - Don't copy the behavior and customs of this world but let God transform you into a new person by changing the way you think. Then you will learn to know God's will for you which is good and pleasing and perfect.

So, here are three steps to add to the transformation process. These things will work in the renewing of your thought life.

1. Forgiveness

You have to forgive the ones who hurt you the most. This doesn't mean you need to hear them say they are sorry. The truth is, you probably won't ever hear that from them. Forgiveness equals freedom. Not forgiving equals imprisonment. And the person who hurt you is holding the key. You can't have freedom and be bitter. And scripture says in multiple places that you should forgive those who hurt you, just as the Lord has forgiven you.

Ephesians 4:32 NIV- Be kind and compassionate to one another, forgiving each other, just as in Christ God forgave you.

2. Find ways that God can use your pain.

We have to come to the conclusion that life happened and there isn't anything we can do to change it. We can look back in some of the darkest times and see God never left us. You can even see how God used it to shape who we are today! When we realize that it can all serve a higher purpose, we can let go of the pain. Our story isn't just for us. It is for other people. It declares the goodness of God. When you know that your story is helping someone else, it gives it a new meaning. God can use every evil thing that happened to us for His good and His glory!

Romans 8:28 NIV - And we know that in all things God works for the good of those who love Him, whom have been called according to his purpose.

3. Forget about it.

We bring the past into the present because we won't stop thinking about what happened to us. We replay it over and over then wonder why it still haunts us. You have to forget about it. Clear the thoughts that replay in your mind that hinder us moving forward into who we are called to be. You never become who you are really meant to be if you keep holding on to who you used to be.

So, what in your life is a pile of ashes? Are you ready to release it and let it go? You have to let the past be the past because there is no room for it in the present.

PART II

These are practical steps that you can walk out after the initial transformation, but we need to go a little deeper into practical step number one. It is the most vital action required on our part: forgiveness. Forgiveness is very tricky, but it must be a part of your journey because it will play a huge part in your freedom. You have to forgive the ones that haven't said "I'm sorry." Like I said before, they may never apologize. It takes a lot of courage and stripping away of pride to go back and apologize to someone, so it doesn't happen as often as it should. But, it doesn't matter in this case. You have to forgive the people who did the unthinkable things to you. The parent who abandoned you, the kids who bullied you, the brother who raped you, the person who introduced you to drugs. Anyone that has hurt you or wronged you in any way, you have to forgive them. You can hole yourself up in the prison of unforgiveness, but that doesn't help you, and it doesn't really hurt them. That is the truth of the matter. You holding onto it hurts you more than it hurts them. You can't change what happened, but you can decide if it is going to control you.

Now, let me make sure I am clear on this. You don't have to post it to social media, you don't have to call them up, and you definitely don't have to see them to forgive them. They don't need to know you have forgiven them. Like I said before, they probably aren't holding onto the fact that you haven't forgiven them. I am sure they aren't thinking about it at all. Just forgive them in your heart and let go of the bitterness. On the other side of this, if you are truly feeling led by the Spirit to let this person know you have forgiven them, then by all means, do it the way the Spirit leads you. But, know that there is likely a lesson in it for you somewhere. For example, at one of my many jobs when I was wild, I had a boss who was married. One day at work, he stuck his hands down my shirt. I walked out of that job right then and never went back. Then I replayed that moment of hurt over and over again. About two years into my transformation, I had a sudden thought of this man and my heart was heavy for him. That thought brought me to tears and God began to show me what I had done to encourage the situation. Every day I would come to work in my extra-slutty clothes and I would flirt with all of the guys, including him. I knew that I was never going to cross that line (because remember, I didn't want to be a home-wrecker), but how was this guy supposed to know that? Does that excuse what he did? No. But, that just means that I shared some of the responsibility. So, when God shed His light on my faults, I felt compelled to write this guy a letter, telling him everything that God had done in my life, and also to apologize to him. I know, you are probably shaking your head at me right now. But, that is how God works sometimes. When God has you do something, there is a lesson for you somewhere in there. So, I am talking to you about forgiveness, while also acknowledging that I needed to apologize. There is an important lesson for us embedded in forgiveness: humility. If we are too prideful to apologize, then we need to check and see if we are too prideful to cut the rope we have around the other person's neck. But, as I said, choosing to not forgive is only choking you out of an abundant life, not them. Let your past be your past and start by forgiving, so that you can find peace in this area.

Ephesians 4:31-32 NIV- Get rid of all bitterness, rage, anger, harsh words, and slander, as well as all types of evil behavior. Instead, be kind to each other, tenderhearted, forgiving one another, just as God through Christ has forgiven you.

So, you may be thinking, "Jessica, I don't have an issue with forgiveness." Okay, maybe you don't. But, can I be real with you? Maybe you have an issue with self-pity. You may just think it is everyone else's fault. You may have unrealistic expectations, so stop blaming everyone else for your misery. Stop telling everyone you meet how someone else hurt you. I fully understand that people need to talk some things out to process the pain, but if you tell more than three people about it, you aren't looking for help, you are looking for attention. You are looking for someone to just feel sorry for you.

You have to evaluate the people you are talking to. Are they someone that can actually help you in your situation? Or are they someone who is sowing a negative seed into your misery? Are they fueling your rage or are they speaking life, encouragement, and wisdom over your situation? If they aren't doing the latter part of that question, then you need to stop talking to them about it. Y'all didn't know I was going to get this real, did you? Well, I'm about to go even deeper. Let's take a look at the patterns of your life. Do you keep getting hurt the same way over and over, just by different people? What is the common factor in that statement? It's you. Earlier in the book we talked about it not being our fault, and at that point, that was very much the case! But at some point in our lives, some of our pain does become our fault because we get to a place where we have the chance to change it, and rather than change it, we wallow in it. So, be honest with yourself. Search and see if you are the problem. If you are just looking for people to hurt you, or provoking the pain, it's time to get over yourself and stop waiting for someone to feel sorry for you. I know this was all very forward, but I don't believe growth comes with a sugary coating. If we are going to change, we have to face some hard facts about ourselves too.

Philippians 3:13 NLT - No, dear brothers and sisters, I have not achieved it, but I focus on this one thing: Forgetting the past and looking forward to what lies ahead.

You've heard the saying, "there are many layers to an onion, and you just have to keep peeling." Well, that is forgiveness. It has many layers and steps. So, now we move on to forgiving yourself. You have to forgive yourself for all that you have done. You can't love yourself if you hate yourself, and you can't love others or receive love if you don't love yourself. Sometimes you just have to say, "I was just young and dumb." And that's okay. We are all young and dumb at some point. There is no person who has not made poor choices in their life, other than Jesus. The Lord says there is no condemnation for those who are in Christ, so stop rehashing all of your mistakes and love the person that you are becoming. Seriously, what good does rehashing do? The only reason that you should be bringing up your mistakes is if you are trying to use them to teach someone else not to make them. Otherwise, there is no reason to bring it up. You are worthy of self-love because God created you in His image. I heard it somewhere, "How we treat creation is a reflection of how we think about the One who created it." Well, Christ created us, so remember that and be kind to yourself. How will we ever believe the promises of God that speak to our worth and value, if we don't believe we are worthy or valuable because of our past? So, always, when you are speaking to yourself, keep in mind the One who created you and what His word says about you.

Romans 8:1-2 NIV- Therefore, there is now no condemnation for those who are in Christ Jesus, because through Christ Jesus the law of the Spirit who gives life has set you free from the law of sin and death.

And another layer to forgiveness is: forgiveness doesn't mean you have to let the person who hurt you back into your life. I forgave my mom 1,000 times, but if I try to have a relationship with her, she will just give me another reason to have to forgive her 1,001 times. Some people don't change their lives, so they don't have to have a spot in your new life. This doesn't make you a bad person and it doesn't mean that you haven't forgiven them. You just have to know what a healthy boundary or relationship looks like with those people. If having a relationship with them hinders you from moving forward, then it's not healthy for you. And let me just tell you, those people will have a problem with it, too. They will probably have a negative opinion about your choice to separate yourself from them, but that is just it. That is their opinion. You know what God has for you. They don't know what God has for you.

Another example of this in my life would be my loyalty to my family. They are my blood, but I still had to separate myself from them. Not because I am better than them, or because I developed a "holier than thou" mentality when I became a Christian. No, it was because they didn't actually want me to change. Of course they said things like, "Oh, Jessica thinks she is better than us," or, "Jessica really thinks she is something now that she married into money." Again, that was not the case for me, and should not be the case for you. If you are cutting them out of your life for this reason, then you need to re-evaluate your heart.

As I mentioned above, I have forgiven my mom, but I choose not to be in a relationship with her. I never had a true relationship with her, but there were times when she would want to be in my life. It would be fine for a while, but then her dysfunction would always find its way back into our lives. What I kept thinking every time was how Jon didn't deserve it. He didn't deserve them destroying me, his wife, every six months. So, I cut ties right after our wedding. I had to remove the person who started my cycle of rejection. I promise you, Satan will use the people closest to you to keep you from reaching your destiny. I had to cut ties with my brother, too. They hated me for it, but I had to do what was healthy for me and my family.

Beyond family, you will have friends that you have had your whole life who won't understand when God transforms you. Y'all remember my best girlfriend, Jennifer? We were "Jenn and Juice" back then, and we were inseparable. She is the friend I lived with for a short period after I had Ozzie. I always felt like they were kind of my saving grace. She was married to a man named Don, and he was always a huge part of our lives, and our parties. When I met Jon and surrendered my life to Jesus, I knew that I couldn't be around Jennifer and Don if I wanted to stay faithful. You see, when I was around them, I would have flashbacks of those drunken nights when we would all be sleeping around with everyone. Even talking on the phone with Jennifer brought back those memories, and I didn't want to remember that time. I will spare you the details, but you can imagine the extent of the things I heard. But, I still loved Jennifer so much. They were my family. I didn't know how I was going to just remove her from my life after decades of friendship, but I knew that I had to. It wouldn't be easy.

It was actually one of the hardest parts of my transformation. Cutting ties with Don and Jennifer was harder than my own actual family. And they, for sure, didn't understand why it was happening. I remember it like it was yesterday, Don called and left the worst voicemail on my answering machine. In today's world they would have plastered it all over social media. He called me plenty of ugly names and gave their opinion on reasons why they thought I was cutting them out of my life. But, all of it was a lie! They were lies that Satan wanted me to believe instead of the truth that I knew. So, to say the least, Jon and I had some battles to fight our first year of marriage that had nothing to do with us. I was trying to figure out how to become a new creation in Christ, while hearing how wrong I was for doing it, but still feeling like I was on my way to be exactly the person I had always dreamed of becoming.

Thirteen

TIME TO RISE

It is time to rise above the cards you have been dealt. It is time to rise above what your family has done to you. It is time to rise above and become more than what everyone expected you to be. Everyone else may be saying that you are already dead and there is no place for hope, but just like me, you can rise up out of the ashes and be turned into something beautiful. Here are some truths that I think will be vital to your walk. They will help you to rise above it all.

1. It is time to rise in our marriages.

I would be lying to you if I told you that Jon and I haven't had any battles to face in fifteen years of marriage. The pain I experienced was real, and it can still try to creep its way into my world sometimes. It doesn't control me, but there are scars that can still be seen. I am so thankful that God chose to give me a husband that loves me despite all of my scars. To rise in our marriage means dying to ourselves for their sake, just like we are to die to ourselves for Jesus. We are to live selflessly, give selflessly, and love selflessly. We have to work, y'all. Even with Jesus in the center, marriage isn't easy. But it is so rewarding when we learn how to serve, love, and give grace to our spouse. Divorce is a vicious cycle. You have the power to stop it from happening to you.

2. It is time to rise above what the world says about you.

The world will say there is no hope. The world will say that you can't make it. The world will tell you that you can't change. The world will make itself look more glamorous. It will look easier to be of the world, rather than just in it. Don't listen to the world! Rise up, my friend! I have shared my life with you! I hope that it has given you a new hope that your story can be different, too! Your situation isn't dead. It is not final. The cross has the final word! Take Jesus' hand, get up, and begin to change!

Mark 5:39-42 NIV- He went in and said to them, "Why all this commotion and wailing? The child is not dead but asleep." But they laughed at him. After he put them all out, he took the child's father and mother and the disciples who were with him, and went in where the child was. He took her by the hand and said to her, "Talitha koum!" (which means "Little girl, I say to you, get up!"). Immediately the girl stood up and began to walk around (she was twelve years old). At this they were completely astonished.

3. It is time to rise, ask for wisdom, and gain a new perspective.

God's word is the one thing that is stable enough to keep us centered. His word is our lamp in life. Read the Word and search for the wisdom in it. Then, let it change your perspective. Life isn't always roses. Even in this moment, I could be pissed and feel like my husband isn't supporting me in my book writing, or I could be thankful that he works around the clock so that I can be a stay-at-home mom and write this book. See, perspective is everything. When it is shifted in the right direction, your mood and your motivation is instantly elevated.

James 1:5 NLT- If you need wisdom, ask our generous God, and He will give it to you. He will not rebuke you for asking.

Proverbs 4:7 NLT- Getting wisdom is the wisest thing you can do! And whatever else you do, develop good judgment.

4. It is time to rise and defeat the enemy.

Satan's deception tastes sweet. He doesn't come out and tempt us with something we are expecting. No, he is smart, and patient, and very sly. He will come with a slightly twisted version of the truth, so that it still sounds good to us. He lures us in by making us think there is something in it for us. Like we will gain something. There is so much to unpack here. The enemy is on the prowl looking for someone to devour. Is he going to get you? Or are you going to be ahead of the game? Lions are not that fast, they are just strategic. They are patient in studying their prey. They will wait for the perfect opportunity to attack. The enemy is like this. He knows what we like and where we like to spend our time. He knows our weak spots. He will sit and wait until you let your guard down, and then he attacks. Isn't that just peaches? So, where does he attack us the most? I am glad you asked. He attacks us most in our minds. We assume things that aren't true. We believe things that aren't real. We begin to isolate ourselves from people who can actually help us. He gets in your mind and makes you think you aren't good enough, smart enough, rich enough, pretty enough, lucky enough, or worthy of anything good that God has for you. He can even make you think that the bad things he is actually causing are from God. Do not believe him! God has plans to prosper you, not to harm you!

Jeremiah 29:11 NIV- "For I know the plans I have for you," declares the Lord, "Plans to prosper you and not to a harm you, plans to give you hope and a future."

John 12:31 NLT- "The time for judging this world has come, when Satan, the ruler of this world, will be cast out."

1 Peter 5:8 NIV- Be alert and of sober mind. Your enemy, the devil, prowls around like a roaring lion, looking for someone to devour.

5. It is time to rise above social media.

The enemy uses social media as a tool to make us discontent and jealous, self-absorbed yet feeling less-than. I fully believe that social media can be used as a tool for God and His goodness and glory, but Satan currently has his hooks in a lot of people through social media. Let me just tell you, social media doesn't have to control you! You may not have a drug addiction, but chances are, you have a social media addiction. I would bet that some of you are addicted to how many likes you can get and what people think about your life. You want it to look like you have a more perfect life than you actually do. Trust me, I know this all too well. Honestly, how can we expect to think clearly when we are filling our minds with social media standards?

For the sake of these next few lines, everywhere I type the word "you," insert "social media" into its place. You control my life. You are the reason I think my life has to be a certain way. You make me feel less-than when I am following my purpose. You take away time with my kids and my spouse because you are a distraction. You make me feel like I have to capture every moment and post about it, otherwise, I will look and feel uncool. You make me feel like I have a lot of friends, but when I take a hiatus, I don't hear from anyone. You put me in a bad mood when people want to talk to me, because all I want to do is scroll through. You are the first thing I do before my feet ever hit the ground.

All of these things sound like an addiction to me. It is healthy and necessary to take social media breaks every once and a while. We need to look up from our devices and enjoy the moment! Don't get me wrong here, I love social media. For all of its bad, there is a lot of good that it can do. It lends the opportunity to reach and affect people you may never otherwise meet. I just don't want anything to have more control of my life than I have over myself, so I will take a break and allow my heart to realign with God's standards and the beauty that He has surrounded me with.

Romans 12:2 NLT- Don't copy the behavior and customs of this world, but let God transform you into a new person by changing the way you think. Then you will learn to know God's will for you, which is good and pleasing and perfect.

6. It is time to rise above fear.

Fear is another tactic that the devil uses to hold us back. He uses it to attack and destroy the people we are called to be. So much of what God has for us is just on the other side of our fear.

John 14:27 NIV- "Peace I leave with you; my peace I give you. I do not give to you as the world gives. Do not let your hearts be troubled and do not be afraid."

To say "do not let" means that we have a choice! We have the choice to be afraid or be brave. We have the choice to stay in our comfort zone or get out of the boat. What if we used the energy that fear produces and put it into living life to the fullest? What do you have to be afraid of? Are you afraid of what people will think about you or your choice? Stop. Are you afraid to fail? Stop. Are you afraid of rejection? Stop. Do not be afraid of these things, because these things do not matter. What matters is that you stepped out in faith, and if it doesn't work out the first time, then you will rise and step out again. Fear is a choice. What would you do if you weren't afraid? Think on that and write it down. Then work through your list and see all of the amazing things you can accomplish when you step out in faith.

Joshua 1:9 NIV - Have I not commanded you? Be strong and courageous. Do not be afraid; do not be discouraged, for the Lord your God will be with you wherever you go.

2 Timothy 1:7 NIV- For the Spirit God gave us does not make us timid, but gives us power, love, and self-discipline.

Psalm 56:3 NIV- When I am afraid, I put my trust in you.

7. It is time to rise and speak positively over your life.

Our words are so powerful. We have the ability to kill or give life with just our words. For twenty-two years, I spoke death over myself. We have talked about this throughout the whole book, but it begins in your mind. What you think is what you speak. So, what is it that you speak over your life? Do you speak death and negativity? Or do you speak life and victory? It should definitely be the latter of those. I understand if you don't know how to speak life over yourself. Probably because you haven't had anyone set that example for you. I am going to give you a little list of things that you can begin to speak over yourself. I challenge you to commit to doing this for even three days and see how it makes you feel.

- Thank you Lord for the very breath you gave me.
- Thank you Lord that with every step I take, you have gone before me.
- I am fearfully and wonderfully made.
- I was created in Your image.
- No weapon formed against me shall prosper.
- Thank you for my story because it will bring hope to others.
- The battle is won. Jesus, my victory is in you!

Proverbs 18:21 MSG- Words kill, words give life; they're either poison or fruit—
you choose.

Proverbs 12:18 NIV- The words of the reckless pierce like swords, but the tongue of the wise brings healing.

Proverbs 16:24 NIV- Gracious words are a honeycomb, sweet to the soul and healing to the bones.

When you make the choice to rise up, you may not succeed in every single step, every single day. I am still a work in progress, y'all. But, I promise I will continue to work on rising up. I hope you will make that promise to yourself, too.

Fourteen

CHOSEN

In 2007, I was chosen as a contestant in a celebrity look-alike contest. I was chosen because I looked like Martina McBride. I was flown out to California, given a "celebrity style" makeover, and was photographed for the Celebrity 101 Hairstyle magazine. For this contest, three of us were chosen and one out of the three would be on the cover of the magazine. I knew it was going to be me. I don't say that to be prideful, but of the three of us, I did look most like Martina McBride. The reason I say I knew it would be me is because God was paving the way for me to have the desires of my heart. If you remember, there was a time when this small town girl wanted to be a model, but was going about it the world's way and with the wrong intent. We know that didn't turn out well for me. I know this is such a vain desire, but I felt like God had given me this look and He was going to pick me. Since He has turned my life around, that's how I've walked. Confident. I can confidently know that whatever He chooses me for, it will happen even if I am not qualified according to the world's standards. All because He chose me. And let me tell you something, He chose you too. Y'all, God chose me to write this book and I am the least qualified person in this world to write. But, I am willing to do what He has called me to do and I will be able to do it with His help.

Philippians 4:13 NIV- I can do all this through Christ who gives me strength.

When you come from a place of knowing you are chosen, your confidence goes up, and people are attracted to confident people. Good things start happening for you.

Dreams and desires that you have tucked away start to come to life. These statements are true, but there is always another edge to the sword. Just because you are chosen, doesn't mean you are accepted. Jesus accepts everyone, but the church isn't always so kind and gracious. The church will hinder you if you let it.

We need to talk about the raw and real offense that happens in church. More appropriately described for some places as religious people and legalism. When you decide to turn away from your old life, you will need to find a church home. You will need to have a place and a community of people that will point you to Jesus and challenge you to grow in your spiritual relationship with Christ. That is why we have to talk about this.

Jon and I had always been involved in the local church. When we first got married we went to a Baptist Church in Texarkana. This is where we were going while I was transforming. This is where I got a foundation of scripture. But then we moved to Dallas and began attending a church where we learned how to serve the house and how to love people. Now, when we moved to Dallas I knew I was called to the ministry. I put a pause on my career to pursue where God was calling me. Our church held a conference and the guest speaker began talking about rural America. He was from a small town and felt called to transform religion in small communities. This spoke straight to my heart. After leaving that day, I went home and told Jon what God had shown me. I shared what I felt like I was called to do, and that was to go back to the small towns like I had grown up in. Not to necessarily change religion like the speaker, but to bring hope to the hopeless. I wanted to find girls that were hopeless like I was and share my story with them. I wanted to bring them the hope that I had found. I started a nonprofit called Just Fabulous Events. We would have worship music, a fashion show, and makeovers; it was a time for girls to have safe, innocent fun and learn about their worth and value. We even had events around prom season and the organization collected prom dresses to disburse at the events. Girls showed up at these events and left with more than a makeover and a new cute dress. They would look in the mirror and talk about how beautiful they felt. They would leave with purpose and hope, knowing that they didn't have to end up like everyone else in their community.

Everything was going great with the organization, but then we ran into a little misunderstanding with the church. I was passionate about not mixing my non-profit with volunteering at the church. It all came to a head when they thought I was handing out flyers for one of my events. Someone approached me and told me that I couldn't do that. Instantly, my heart sank. I felt like someone had taken a baseball bat to my knees and knocked my feet out from under me. This accusation really wrecked me. I felt like my integrity had been brought into question by people I highly respected. In the present moment of offense, what were we to do? Leave and never go back? No. We talked about how leaving offended would affect us more than staying, so we gave it almost a year before we felt God release us from that church.

From there we began the hunt. Since there was a church on every corner in Dallas, we didn't expect it to be too difficult. It was way harder than we anticipated. We would walk into churches and no one would speak to us. This happened over and over again. Walking in and feeling likes strangers that were not welcome. One time (and this is kind of comical), we heard about a church plant that was a part of a church we had already attended once. We went, and there were like twelve people total. The silence and stares were unbearable and so uncomfortable. So, we kept going to a few others and felt so discouraged. We began to question whether or not God truly said it was okay for us to leave our last church home. Jon's brother, Ben, had a roommate who was working for a church in Austin. He knew we were looking for a church home and told us to check out a new church plant that a couple from the Austin church was starting in Dallas. Are you serious? After the last "church plant" experience? No, thank you! But, nothing else was working out, so we got online and looked up the couple who were coming to Dallas to plant this church. Whoa, we were impressed by their heart for Dallas and their heart for people! We felt an instant pull to give it a shot.

We got the boys all dressed up in their colorful skinny jeans and plaid shirts.

It was time to go check this church out. At the time, they were meeting in a movie theater, so initially we weren't super confident that this would be our church home. We pulled into the parking lot, looked around, then looked at each other and said, "Walk straight in and straight out." We didn't want to talk to anybody or get involved. We were scarred from our previous church. We were healed, but still sensitive. We walked up to the outside doors and there were people standing there, holding the doors open, and welcoming us in. They said, "Hi! We are so glad you are here!" They directed us to the theater where we would be having "church." We had to ride up the escalator and it felt like we were moving in slow motion. At the top there were people waiting to embrace you with a hug that would cut off your air supply. They were intense, but in a good way. Every few steps there was someone welcoming us, giving us hugs, helping us with the kids, or leading us to our seats. It felt like there were so many people, but really there were only about one hundred people at the time. We made it to our seats as worship was starting. From the first note sang, the Holy Spirit fell on us! My hands immediately wanted to raise in full surrender. I never wanted the songs to end. Though there were only one hundred of us, it was like the worship leader was leading thousands of us in praise. Everything felt so perfect. I knew that it had been covered in prayer and God was breathing directly on this place.

Then, it was the pastor's turn. We had seen him in the video; a tall African-American man, full of life and joy. He was ready to share Jesus with every single one in that room. Key word being "one." We said that we were going to slip in and slip out. Well, we didn't just slip in, so I don't know why we thought we could just slip out. Before we knew it, the pastor had come up and talked to us as if we were the only ones he was there to minister to. This was already crazy to us, because in our old church you never saw the pastor in the lobby talking to the members. Which to a point I understand for safety, but nonetheless, it was something that we craved. We wanted to be covered by our pastors. We wanted to get to know them on a personal level. When we made it outside, we took a family photo because I told Jon, "We will want to remember this if this becomes our church home." I don't know why we didn't just come out and say it right then and there. This was our church home. We got in the car and didn't say a word, mostly because we didn't have to; you could just read it all over our faces. This was our home. We had found the place where we would plant our roots and grow forever.

So, we went back the next week and the Pastor, Pastor Earl, remembered our names. That did us in. We were serving within a few weeks! On their website video, they said this church was going to be a church like the world had never seen before. After being there even just one time, we believed it. Honestly, we never thought we had that much growing left to do or that God wanted to transform us anymore. Can anyone say, "prideful much?" Man, God has used this church to change our lives, to challenge us, to help us love people more, and give us a place to love the broken. Our mission statement is "On Earth as it is in Heaven." That is literally what we have witnessed in the six years of being there. Sundays now consist of three services and about three thousand people. We have a women's ministry called Sisterhood. It changes the way women have relationships with each other. It changes the way we look at each other and the way we look at ourselves. Our pastor's wife, Pastor Oneka, has a heart for the one. She loved the one when there was one hundred, and she loves the one when there are thousands. You could call us a "megachurch" because of our growth, but our pastors don't like to call it that. Their heart hasn't changed. You can still find them in the lobby between services, getting to know the people who come to the church. What has been even more beautiful to watch is the way they raise their family. We live in the same suburb as them, and we get to watch them at school and sporting events. They are the same people at home as they are when they are leading from the platform. Honor and humility run through their veins. I have never seen a wife respect her husband more, cheer for him more, or pray for him more. The family comes before the church or outside speaking engagements. Our church is going to change the way other people do church. They will learn from our pastors on how to love and lead. Our pastors support us in everything. They believe in us more than we believe in ourselves sometimes. Even in writing this book. Pastor Oneka has continuously asked me about its progress and says that she cannot wait to hand it out. Wow! We are in such a blessed season because of the amazing community we have in our church home. I say all of this because I am honored to be on this journey with them. My family was chosen by God to be a part of this church, but we weren't just chosen by God, we were accepted by the Pastors and the members of the church. And now, we are reaching the chosen. Like the Shepherd, we are leaving the ninety-nine in search of the lost one.

Luke 15:4 NIV- "Suppose one of you has a hundred sheep and loses one of them. Doesn't he leave the ninety-nine in the open country and go after the lost sheep until he finds it?"

Matthew 6:9-10 NIV- "This, then, is how you should pray; Our Father in Heaven, hallowed be your name, your Kingdom come, your will be done, on Earth as it is in Heaven."

Shoreline City Creed

I am loved by God

I cannot earn it

I cannot lose it

In Christ I am forgiven

And made brand new

I live with passion and purpose

I am empowered by the Spirit

To be the church in the World

And to live for the Glory of God

Fifteen
WORTH THE PAIN
PART I

I get to go back to small towns and find girls like me and deal them some hope, which makes all of my pain worth it. But more than that, I have become the mom that I always wanted. It is worth the pain. I have had the honor of being called "wife" by the most amazing man for fifteen years. It is worth the pain. Being called to be a pastor to the broken makes it all worth it. I know it is hard to see through the pain right now, but trust me, it will be worth it one day if you don't give up. You will only fail and it will never be worth anything if you quit. I wanted this book to end on a story that brings it full circle. So, we are about to go out with a bang here!

At the beginning of 2016, in the middle of a growing season in our church, as I am ministering to people, I got the urge to adopt. This feeling literally came over me so strongly, I can't accurately describe it. I am crazy enough to believe that social media would help me find a daughter. I wanted a daughter so badly. I love my boys, but I wanted to have a daughter to raise. So, I posted about wanting to adopt a daughter, and within three hours I had a message from someone. This person shared with me that the mom was a drug addict and was using while pregnant. She also had a few other kids already that she wasn't raising. So, I begin the search. She was from my hometown and was married to a boy that I went to school with, although he was in jail. Some people even said that my brother was the one who had gotten her pregnant. So, I was like, "Okay God, you laid it on my heart to post to Facebook, now there is a baby, and it is my brother's?" I can't make this stuff up, people! So, I called around and she hadn't even been to the doctor to know the sex of the baby. She was actually going that following Tuesday, and I felt in my heart right then; if this baby was a girl, she would be my daughter. It just so happened that this baby was, in fact, a little girl. So, I started to do some asking around and found out where they lived. They did not have a phone, so I couldn't call them. I asked Jon to drive me there. Being the amazing man that he is, there was no hesitation. We went to the store and I bought a bunch of things for the mom and the baby. Then, I went a step further and wrote the baby a letter. We began to drive to their trailer. Remember, we couldn't contact them, so they weren't expecting us. I knew people had said she originally wanted to give this baby up, but I didn't know what to expect in this moment. Here we were, essentially strangers, coming to her trailer to ask her to give us her baby. We make it there, drive up, and it is completely dark. As we walked up to the door, my heart was pounding. I was relieved when the guy I had gone to school with opened the door. He had recently been released from prison. We walked in the house, and it was so dirty. Piles of trash everywhere, a mattress on the living room floor, and no electricity. And to top it off, this nine-months-pregnant woman was sitting there eating McDonald's. My heart became heavy with compassion for her life. I wanted right then to tell her everything she could do to transform her life. But, I knew I couldn't start the conversation with that. Instead, it started out with small talk. We gave her the gift basket and the letter that I had written. We shared how we would provide for this little girl and that she wouldn't have anything to worry about. We shared our dream of adopting her. Then she said the words my heart did not want to hear. She said that if it were earlier in the pregnancy, she might have been able to go through with it, but she didn't think she could do it now. I didn't understand. *What? You mean you don't think you could let this child come home with a family that wasn't on drugs? You can't let her come home to a place that has electricity?* Nonetheless, in the midst of all my disappointment, I knew that it would be okay and I had to respect her choice. So, I prayed over her and the baby and we left. I thought (and hoped) she would change her mind, but that wasn't the case. The baby was born, and rumors were, that sweet baby girl tested positive for drugs and Child Protective Services got involved. But, no one ever called us to come get her. I knew that God was protecting us and working out His own perfect plan.

So, three weeks after this baby girl was born, I found out that I was pregnant! Did you see that coming at all? Man, we didn't. God had bigger plans than we could have ever dreamed. I was so excited to tell Jon when he got home from work. My first sentence was, "Well, we are going to need a suburban." We were so happy and we knew deep down that God was giving us our very own little girl. He was fulfilling the desires of our heart. This little girl already had a call on her life, even as she was in my womb, so you can bet the devil came at us hard. We were not prepared for the battle ahead.

Within the first few weeks, I had my first bleeding episode and symptoms of a miscarriage. We called the doctor and they told us to prepare for the loss. How do you prepare for something like that? God had blessed us with this precious life and we didn't want to see it ripped away from us in an instant. Thankfully, the symptoms went away and the baby was fine. We were so happy again, but it was short lived. My second episode came, and this time the symptoms were much worse; I bled for seventeen days. On the seventeenth day, something much worse happened. I can't go into the details, but we thought for sure we had miscarried. We immediately left for the doctor's office. We didn't speak the entire car ride. This was the most sadness we had ever felt.

We were so cold when we finally made it to the doctor's office. We were prepared to get the sonogram over with and begin the grieving process. But, the moment the doctor touched my stomach, we heard the heartbeat. Everyone in the room was in complete shock. How is this possible? God put His arms around our precious miracle and nothing would harm this baby. As relieving as this moment was, I couldn't recover emotionally. I actually fell into a pit that I hadn't been in since I gave my life to Christ. It was a feeling of hopelessness, like I would still eventually lose the baby. I couldn't be happy or get excited for this baby anymore. Actually, at this time, we didn't know for sure the sex of the baby. We only knew what we felt it would be in our heart. I became very protective of my heart. I began to put up walls because I thought, "If something is going to happen, I am going to block my heart from the pain." Well, at the next appointment, we found out the gender. And just as we felt it would be, it was a perfect little girl. That moment was unreal. I had hoped to hear those words when I was pregnant with my first child. I just wanted redemption. I wanted to raise a princess who would be protected and happy. I wanted to raise a daughter that would never hurt the way that I did. I know that I can't protect her from all of the brokenness in the world, but I can protect her from abandonment and rejection by never leaving her side. The remainder of the pregnancy had its rough patches, but nothing like the beginning.

Our beautiful daughter, Jazzlin Faith Marie Youngblood, came into this world on October 24, 2016. After having her, I was transformed all over again. As dark as the pregnancy was, her birth was like seeing a rainbow after the storm. A new hope had risen in my soul, a kind that I had never felt. You see, being a mom to the boys, I was still caught up in my own kind of selfishness. Don't get me wrong, I was good to them. They were always fed, clothed, clean, and taken to church, but I worked a lot, and was glad to. Having my daughter was different. I was older, wiser, and had gone through such a fight to get her here that I was determined to enjoy every moment I had with her. I was going to enjoy waking up in the middle of the night. I was going to enjoying changing dirty diapers. I was going be the loving, nurturing mom that I didn't have. I am by no means perfect, but I did get that right this year. I did it right with her. As I write this last chapter, she is turning one, and I can tell you without a shadow of a doubt, I have no regrets for this past year. Jazzie has changed me.

God, in all of His goodness, gave me a daughter. He gave me another level of redemption. When I look at my daughter, I think, "How could my mom have left me?" But I know that her pain took her in a different direction than mine. But, I will say this with the utmost assurance: that curse is broken in my family. My kids will never be saying, "How could she leave us?" Instead, they will say, "Stop, Mom. You are embarrassing me!"

PART II

I want this book to come out and reach you. I want it to find its way into the deepest, darkest, hardest parts of your mind, heart, and soul. I held nothing back because I want you to know that there is no place too far, no pit too deep, no mountain too steep that can keep God from you if you reach out to Him. I hope y'all read this and know that God is no respecter of persons and what He has done for me, He can do in your life. It's His grace. And it is worth going through all of the pain to get what God has for you.

Psalm 34:18 MSG- If your heart is broken, you'll find God right there; if you're kicked in the gut, He'll help you catch your breath.

Psalm 147:3 NLT- He heals the brokenhearted and bandages their wounds.

Mark 5:34 NIV- He said to her, "Daughter, your faith has healed you. Go in peace and be freed from your suffering."

"Worth the pain" is truly a testament to God's word when it says that He works all things out for good. I can see clearly now that He was always there. While I was drowning in the sea of despair, all I had to do was reach my hand up and He was right there waiting for me. Surrender is sweet. He took it all upon His shoulders so I wouldn't have to bear it any longer. If you are going to have a life worth living, you are going to have to walk through some pain. Just please, don't give up right before your breakthrough!

James 1:2-4 NIV- Consider it pure joy, my brothers and sisters, whenever you face trials of many kinds, because you know that the testing of your faith produces perseverance. Let perseverance finish its work so that you may be mature and complete, lacking nothing.

I wrote this book for you. Are you at the end of your rope begging for a way out? Maybe you are just utterly exhausted from fighting it all. No matter what your situation, Jesus is calling you. The same God who created the Heavens wants to take away your pain and shower you with His love. If you are ready to surrender it all, ask Jesus into your heart, so that He can be the Ruler of your life. You can pray this prayer:

"Dear Jesus, I ask you to forgive me of all my sins. I admit I've made mistakes. But right now, I give you my heart and my life. Give me the strength and power to live for you. In Jesus' name, Amen."

Now, is my life perfect? No. Is everyday a fairytale? No. But, what I can tell you is that every day I make a choice to surrender. A choice to trust. A choice to believe the best. So no matter where you are as you are reading this (you may be high or in a hi-rise), I am crazy enough to believe that God can grab ahold of your heart and remind you that you are loved, valued, and believed in. And if you are reading this book in faith because you have a loved one who is stuck in this pit, I'm praying that your faith is stirred to not give up on them. Keep believing that God has a plan. And if you are the one who sees yourself in me; I want you to know that you story is not over. It is just about to start. If He did it for me, He can do it for you. It is my prayer that one day you too will be able to say it is worth the pain. Jesus thought that you were worth the pain. He would die for you again if He had to. And I promise, the life He has for you, it is Worth the Pain.

I love you, Mom.

ABOUT THE AUTHOR

Jessica Youngblood was born and raised in the small town of Kirby, Arkansas. Her early life was threatened by meth addiction and suicide. She went from feeling like her life would never turn out any different than generations of family before her, to finding Jesus who radically changed her life! He healed her past, helped her to love her present, and she knows the best is yet to come.

Now she lives in a suburb of Dallas, Texas, with her husband, Jon, raising four children: three boys, Ozzie, Ezra & Zeeland, and a sweet princess, Jazzlin-Faith. Her and her husband serve as pastors at their local church. She loves telling her story to bring hope to the hopeless! This book is her biography. This is her journey from meth to ministry.

Made in the USA
Columbia, SC
26 February 2018